AF397454

Following His Glory

Solomon Aggrey

novum pro

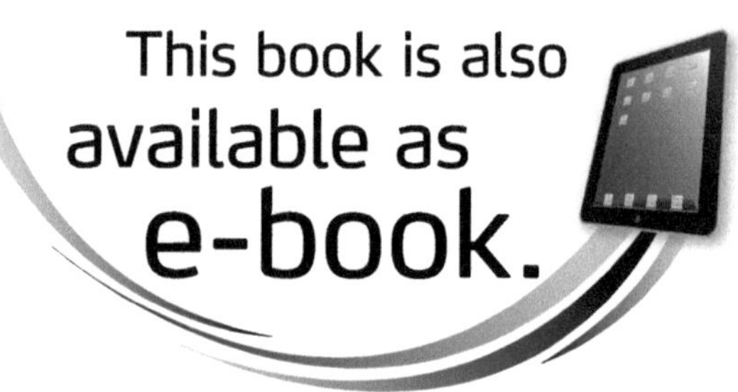

www.novum-publishing.co.uk

© 2021 novum publishing

ISBN 978-3-99107-732-9
Editing: Ashleigh Brassfield, DipEdit
Cover photo:
Rolffimages | Dreamstime.com
Cover design, layout & typesetting:
novum publishing

www.novum-publishing.co.uk

Contents

Introduction

I have been very reluctant to write a book. A solicitor who visited our church said to me, 'Write a book about what you are teaching, and I will help you to edit it.'

I said, 'No!'

Some other members of my church approached me and said, 'Pastor, why don't you put these messages into a book?'

I said, 'No.'

There are millions of Christian books on the market. Some are excellent and are inspired by the Holy Spirit. The moment you begin to read them you feel the imprint of the Holy Spirit. Unfortunately, there are millions of other Christian books, the motives of which are obscure. Some are written for fame, some for prestige, some for money, and some to add the word 'author' to the names of the writers. These books make sense and have Bible quotations, may seem correct theologically, give good advice and have laudable conclusions, but they do not have the life of the Spirit of God. What you get from them is only in the mental realm. They are of the flesh, and what comes of the flesh is flesh, however much they are polished, presented and applauded. They do not work to advance the kingdom of God. The reason why I was reluctant to write a book was because I did not want to birth or add to these millions of flesh books. If it was not in my destiny to write a book, I was not going to force it.

There are also other books, which are released from the kingdom of darkness or empowered from the forces of darkness. They also quote the Holy Bible, and may seem doctrinally correct on the surface, but what they offer is spiritual death. The object of these demonic books is to bring people into darkness, bring confusion, cause people to doubt the Lord and to introduce a different image of Jesus Christ. The moment you begin to read such books, you also begin to lose your zeal and fervour for the Lord. Some of these books unknowingly introduce you to demons and witchcraft. Every Christian needs the help of the Holy Spirit to perceive such crafty counterfeits and choose what to read, especially in the time and age we live in.

Later the Lord suddenly began instructing me to write in dreams and visions. I was still not enthusiastic about it. The Lord sent some other prophets to confirm His word and to tell me to begin to write. I dragged my feet for a long time. OK, what am I going to write? Then the Lord told me in a flash of inspiration that the spirit is the pen. I began then to sense what was in my spirit, and when I put it on paper I was shocked myself at what I began to write; about the glory of the Lord God.

When it comes to anybody writing about the glory or the manifest presence of God, one has to humbly acknowledge his or her complete inadequacy and utter dependence on the Holy Spirit. Even those mighty prophets in the Bible who saw the glory of God found it very difficult to describe it in human language. As I continued to write I felt the Lord's leading to follow the patterns of His glory He had already set in the Old Testament.

When the children of Israel came out of Egypt at the first Passover, the Bible says, 'And the Lord went before them by day in a pillar of cloud to lead the way, and by night in a pillar of fire to give them light, so as to go by day and night. He did not take away the pillar of cloud by day or the pillar of fire by night from before the people.' (Ex 13.21-22). The pillar of cloud and the pillar of fire together was the physical manifestation of God's presence. So, the children of Israel followed the manifest presence of God, which would lead the way and also search out a place for them to camp.

Exodus 40.36-28

The manifest presence of God led them through the Red Sea, through dry and desolate lands, through the wilderness of Sin until they came to the wilderness of Sinai. On Mount Sinai God descended in His glory and spoke to the children of Israel audibly. The children of Israel later said the glory of the Lord was like a consuming fire. God gave them the law and instructed Moses to build a sanctuary so that He could dwell among them. The children of Israel built the tabernacle of the Lord, the centre of which was the Ark of the Covenant located in the most holy place of the tabernacle. On top of the Ark of the Covenant was the mercy seat. It was on the mercy seat the glory of God would appear to speak to the High Priest.

When the children of Israel left Mount Sinai, they followed the glory of the Lord by following the tabernacle. It took them through one camp after another for 40 years, until they reached their destination. In the Moabite plains the children of Israel had to cross the waters of Jordan into their promise. By that time Moses, Aaron and Miriam had died. A new commander and leader, Joshua, was in charge. He instructed the children of Israel:

Do not come near it that you may know the way by which you must go, for you have not passed this way before.'

Joshua 3.3-4

The children of Israel followed the Ark of the Covenant through the waters of Jordan into Canaan; the land of their promise. The land of Canaan 'flowing with milk and honey' was really a symbol of God's dwelling place in heaven which was a place of endless riches and delight. The Israelites had to go through the wilderness for 40 years before crossing over the Jordan into the Promised Land. Had anyone been left behind in the wilderness, he/she would not have survived the heat of the day, the cold in the night, the drought, the famine, and the perils of dangerous animals in the wilderness. 'Following the Glory' was crucial for their journey, their survival and for their promise.

What happened to the children of Israel throughout their journeys until they reached the promise land was a pattern to us. 'Now all these things happened to them as examples, and they were written for our admonition, upon whom the ends of the ages have come.' (1 Corinthians 10.11). All that happened to the children of Israel in the wilderness was a pattern for our time and generation. We too must follow the glory of God if we have to reach our inheritance and destiny. We are going to pass through some difficult, rough, and hard times, persecutions and tribulations. We must also identify and follow the glory of God if we are to survive.

In the end time, the activities of the antichrist system and the corresponding judgement of God will make things impossible in the natural world. The Bible says, 'He who endures to the end shall be saved.' It also says, 'Whoever calls on the name of the Lord shall be saved.' We need to follow the glory of God more in the times we live in. Coming very soon are times when we cannot afford to walk in error and ignorance. We shall need the hand of the Omnipotent, the mind of the Omnipresence and the word of the Omniscience to survive, otherwise we shall lose our promise and even be destroyed.

Yet today, believers know more about gifts of the Holy Spirit and the anointing but know very little about the glory of God. The world has seen the Pentecostal Revival, Evangelical Revival, and the Charismatic Revival. In all of them, there was a measure of the outpouring of the Holy Spirit. We have read books about the glory of God and heard preachers preach about it, but we have come to the point where we need to experience it for ourselves.

I started as an Anglican priest. While praying the heavens opened and I saw a mighty building, like a church. It stayed in my view for about one minute and slowly dissipated. I was not prepared for that. As a normal Anglican priest, I was not quite conversant with such visions then. What is the meaning of this? I began a search for understanding. Perhaps the search for God had begun earlier than I thought, I don't know. But the search for God still continues in my heart. How does one look for and search for an invisible God who is infinitely bigger and greater? How does one begin to search for the Creator who is omniscience, omnipresent and omnipotent? Where does one begin? The search, I realised, must begin within our own hearts. Therefore, our ideas and concepts about God must be true and not only depend on what we have been told or what we have read from books. We should allow the Holy Spirit, who is Spirit of truth, to guide and lead us to our destination, for we don't know the way.

Some Christians speak as though it were easy to enter into God's manifest presence and parley with Him. No! To put the rhetoric aside, the search for God is arduous and requires too much diligence to encourage any casual seeker. It is not for those with the wrong motives; it is for those who are truly serious and prepared to pay any price for an encounter with God. 'And you will seek Me and find Me, when you search for Me with all your heart,' says God through the prophet Jeremiah. The pattern of the journey of the children of Israel gives us clues.

God has guided my hands in many ways. He has led me back to the Old Testament shadows, copies, and patterns and shown me how they relate to the time in which we live. God is holy, not only in the Old Testament but also in the New Testament. He is the same God. Holiness is His nature, His essential self. He cannot do anything without His holiness. In the same way, God is love and He cannot do anything that is not love. So even God's judgements are part of His loving nature and holiness.

God has chosen to guide man to fulfil His original intent. Man, through the first, Adam, decided to declare independence from God, walk away from Him and hide in fear. The Spirit of God therefore left the earth, but God promised to re-send His Spirit through Jesus Christ to guide us back to Him and to our inheritance. Without the Spirit of God, no man can find Him. Religion blossoms because of man's attempt to find God without His help. We must come out of our religious beliefs in order to find God.

The Bible is much deeper than any theologian, any denomination, and any commentator. No one in the flesh has the full understanding and complete answers to all it has to offer mankind. Until we are transformed into Christ's image we shall continue to see only in part and have different views and interpretations of the same thing. Whatever theological bias you hold, and whatever denomination or persuasion you belong to, does not matter to God if you are truly searching for Him. If you are truly seeking and searching for God, then we might be on the same side or in the same boat despite our theological differences.

You are perhaps going to read about something that you won't like; something that would even seem to offend you and your doctrinal viewpoint. You may not like the style and language in which this book has been written. I would not be surprised. Sometimes

I go back to what I had written earlier and wonder, 'Did I really write that?' Yes, the spirit is the pen. I am not writing to satisfy any doctrinal viewpoint; not even my own. If you are looking for something to disagree with or criticise you will find plenty in this book. I don't hold any superior knowledge than what is written in the Holy Scriptures and perhaps what other inspired men of God have written and said. God is still speaking. He has never stopped speaking to those who can hear. Just because it is different from yours does not make it false.

If this book helps you to get a little glimpse of the Lord or helps you to get a little closer to His presence, then its purpose is served. All the glory goes to the Lord, for He only is worthy.

If, on the other hand, I have misinterpreted or misrepresented what the Holy Spirit is saying to me and to the church, I ask you to forgive me. I pray the Holy Spirit to impart to you Himself a true picture of what He wants to say to His church in the unique time in which we find ourselves.

The time in which we live is crucial. There has never been a time like this and there will never be. It is possible we might be the last generation to witness the second coming of the Lord, Jesus Christ. If this is the case, then we have a special and unique assignment to fulfil and we need to prepare ourselves. May God guide your steps to discover and follow His glory in the time in which we live.

Solomon S. Aggrey

Foreword

It is of paramount importance, right from the beginning of this book, to believe and understand that the whole Bible is the word of God. The word of God is not only the New Testament but also the Old Testament. The God of the Old Testament and the God of the New Testament are one and the same. It is a complete lack of understanding of the plan and purpose of God to try to show that the God of the New Testament is better or different from the God of the Old Testament, 'For I am the LORD. I do not change.' (Malachi 3.6).

The Old Testament conceals the will and plans of God, and the New Testament reveals the will and the plans of the same God.

> 'Remember the former things of old, for I am God and there is no other; I am God, and there is none like Me, declaring the end from the beginning, and from the ancient times things that are not yet done, saying, 'My counsel shall stand, and I will do all My pleasure."
>
> Isaiah 46.9-10

It is like God's signature tune, to declare the end from the beginning. There is no other god like Him. If by God's grace the blindness which came over the eyes of nation of Israel in the wilderness is removed from the eyes of many Christians, we will realise that the first few books of the Bible encode the whole message, the gospel of Jesus Christ, the plan and the will of God. It was delivered to the Old Testament saints in shadows, types, and copies. To decode these prophetic messages one need to have an idea about the true meaning of these shadows, types and copies.

Everything God made and did in the world had to conform to the already existing realities and precedents in eternity. An example is the building of the Ark of the Covenant. 'And see to it that you make them according to the pattern which was shown you on the mountain.' The true Ark of the Covenant was revealed when the Word become flesh and dwelt amongst us. In the New Testament one will find a lot of references to the Old Testament because the Old Testament forms the basis for the proper understanding of the New Testament. If one throws away the Old Testament, one has thrown away the foundation and disfigured the complete understanding of the message of God.

Moses, as the mediator and the redeemer of the children of Israel, was a type of Jesus Christ, the true Mediator and Redeemer. The nation of Israel can also be seen as the first nation, a type of New Testament nation, called ecclesia, church. Many of the things that happened to the first nation are reflected more fully in the New Testament.

'So let no one judge you in food or in drink, or regarding a festival or a new moon or Sabbaths, which are a shadow of things to come but the substance is of Christ.'
Colossians 2.16-17

The Old Testament was the shadow. What a powerful shadow! But what is a shadow? The Greek word for shadow is *'skia,'* which means an imperfect copy or a reflection of the true substance. A shadow is an image cast by an object, making a form, a sketch, or an outline of the primary or the original object. The Bible says, 'the substance is of Christ.' Jesus Christ existed before the foundation of the world (Revelations 13.8), and He cast shadows in the Old Testament.

It means the laws, ordinances, statutes, times, seasons and feasts in the Old Testament, as powerful as they were, only presented shadows of the life and ministry of Christ, the anointed one. In other words, the laws, ordinances, statutes, times, seasons and feasts were images of the Lord Jesus Christ concealed, which became revealed in the New Testament. 'And the Word became flesh and dwelt among us, and we beheld His glory, the glory as of the only begotten of the Father, full of grace and truth.'

In the time of the Old Testament, Jesus Christ had not physically come to the earth, and the New Testament was in the future. So how can someone or an object which is not present cast a shadow? The substance or the original substance was already existing in eternity. When the light of God fell on Him, who was already existing in eternity, it cast a shadow in the Old Testament. The Old Testament, then, was pointing to the original intent of God, which was fully revealed by Jesus Christ in the New Testament.

> 'Now all these things happened to them as examples, and they were written for our admonition, upon whom the ends of the ages have come.'
>
> 1 Corinthians 10.11

The reference points of these 'examples' were the experiences the children of Israel went through, especially in their journey to the promised land; the cloud, the glory of God, the wilderness experiences, the signs and the miracles. The Greek word for 'example' is *tupos*. *Tupos* means a type, a constituent element of some reality which is yet to come; a prototype or a preview; that which is yet to be evolved, developed and perfected. So, the events which occurred in the Old Testament, especially to the children of Israel, were types, prototypes and previews of what was to happen to the children of God in the New Testament, the ecclesia (the church).

God also used copies in the Old Testament to point to the heavenly realm and what was to come in the New Testament.

> 'Therefore it was necessary that the **copies** of the things in the heavens should be purified with these, but the heavenly things themselves with better sacrifices than these. For Christ has not entered the holy places made with hands,

*which are **copies** of the true, but into heaven itself, now to appear in the presence of God for us.'*

Hebrews 9.23-24

Two different Greek words are used for the word 'copies.' The first one is *hupodeigma*. It means 'an example or an exhibit for imitation or for warning.' It can be seen as a specimen or a pattern of imitation. KJV uses the word patterns, so it reads, 'Therefore it was necessary that the patterns of things in the heavens,' pointing us to the imitation of the things in heaven. The earthly tabernacle with all its utensils and services, so powerful, was just a copy. So, God hid the knowledge of the heavenly things in the earthly copies in the Old Testament.

He told Moses, 'Let them make me a sanctuary that I may dwell among them. According to all that I show you, that is, the pattern of the tabernacle and the pattern of all its furnishing, just so you shall make it.' (Exodus 25.8-9); so the earthly tabernacle was a copy, a 'type.'

The second Greek word used for 'copies' is '*antitupon*', meaning antitype. It is a combination of two words, *anti*, meaning equivalent or in its stead, and *tupos*, which we have already encountered as meaning a type, prototype, or preview. *Antitupon* is therefore a form or a figure corresponding or representing a type or the prototype. *Antitupon* is a figure answering to and representing a reality or the substance of the 'type.' The 'type' is in the Old Testament and the antitype is in a New Testament. In the Old Testament, God deals with the 'types,' copies, patterns and shadows, and in the New Testament, God deals with the antitype, the original intent and the substance.

With this understanding we can begin straight away to see that what happened to the saints in the Old Testament (like Enoch, Noah, Abraham, and Moses) were really shadows and patterns of what would happen to the New Testament saints. Apostle Paul says categorically in Galatians 3.29, 'And if you are Christ's you are Abraham's seed, and heir according to the promise.'

The glory of God is addressed more in the Old Testament than in the New Testament because in the New Testament the glory of God is first and foremost within us. We are the temples of God. However, the Old Testament gives us more understanding of the nature and the character of the glory of God. Jesus Christ is 'the brightness of God's glory and the express image of His Person.' (Hebrews 1.3). He was the last expression of God which became flesh (John 1.14). So, one cannot know God unless He reveals Him. He said, 'He who has seen Me has seen the Father.' All the shadows, copies, examples, and patterns were fulfilled in Jesus Christ.

Man is created as a pattern of the Ark of the Covenant. We have the spirit, a soul, and live in a body; spirit, soul and body. The glory of God dwelt in the most holy place in the Old Testament. So, the glory of God dwells in the spirit and not in the soul nor in the body. To discover the glory of God in us we have to bypass or go through the body and the soul.

The soul, which is self-conscious, acts like the veil in the tabernacle, to prevent us getting into our spirits. So even though the glory of God and the kingdom of God are within every truly born-again believer, we have still to learn to discover and engage them. I do not believe the soul is bad, but we need to bring our souls in line with our spirits and with God. You see, the children of Israel left Egypt, but Egypt was in their hearts. They had to learn to bring their souls in line with the will and purpose of God before entering the promised land. And this is exactly what we have to do.

God is in us, but we have to learn to discover Him. Many of us behave as if God is not in us, but only in heaven. Until we discover the God in us, we shall not know God, however much we try to substitute His presence with other things. It also means that we shall not be able to influence the world around us. 'Christ in you, the hope of glory.' Unless we turn this hope into a living faith, we still don't know and have not experienced the glory of God. In the last days, discovering and following the glory of God will be crucial to our survival.

CHAPTER 1

The Voice In The Garden

When God finished creating the heaven and the earth and saw that everything was good, He said, 'Let us make man in Our image, according to Our likeness, let them have dominion over the fish of the sea, over the birds of the air and over the cattle, over all the earth and over every creeping thing that creeps on the earth,' (Genesis 1.26). God gave Adam (mankind) dominion over the whole earth. 'For you have made him a little lower than the angels, and You have crowned him with glory and honour. You have made him to have dominion over the works of Your hands; You have put all things under his feet.' (Psalms 8.5-6).

God put Adam in the garden in Eden and told him, 'Of every tree of the garden you may freely eat; but of the tree of the knowledge of good and evil you shall not eat, for in the day that you eat of it you shall surely die.' (Genesis 2.16-17). The devil using the serpent deceived the woman, the wife of Adam. She ate of the tree of the knowledge of good and evil and gave to Adam, her husband to eat. So, they disobeyed God and rebelled against God's word, and declared themselves independent. As a result, the Spirit of God which had taken residence in them left and they lost their oneness with God.

Even though God knew what had happened, He went to the garden in Eden looking for them. 'Where are you?'

Adam and Eve had heard the Voice of God walking in the garden and had hid themselves from His presence (Genesis 3.8). Adam replied, 'I heard Your voice in the garden and I was afraid because I was naked; and I hid myself.'

The rebellion of Adam and his wife had made them naked before God. God did not tell them to hide themselves, but they hid themselves because they could not endure God's presence.

'Who told you that you were naked? Have you eaten from the tree of which I commanded you that you should not eat?'

Adam and his wife, Eve, forfeited their unique relationship and communion with God when they sinned. They lost the image and the likeness of God with which they were created. Adam and Eve acquired a different image, a different constitution, and a different nature. They became of the flesh, no longer guided by God's Spirit but by their own minds, desires and will. Adam and Eve also lost their influence or dominion on earth and the devil took over the dominion of the world.

When Adam and Eve saw they were naked, they covered themselves with fig leaves, but God killed innocent animals and covered them with the tunics, showing them that the way or the platform for direct access to God's presence had changed (Genesis 3.21). The new way was that man would have to come to God and fellowship with Him through the sacrifice of innocent blood. The blood was the life of the animal, so the blood of the innocent animal in principle was exchanged for the death which sin brought. Adam and Eve were driven out of the garden in Eden. All mankind was at the loins of Adam when he sinned, and came out of Adam's fallen nature. So, mankind sinned.

The word of the Psalmist implies that God used to visit Adam and Eve in the Garden in Eden. "What is man that You are mindful of him, and the son of man that You visit him?" (Psalms 8.4). It would not be incorrect to infer that Adam and God were good friends and they used to take walks together in the Garden in Eden, enjoying some time together before Adam's fall. Adam therefore might have seen God face to face or seen a form of God's presence, even though the Bible is silent about it.

The Bible does not tell us of anybody with such a close relationship with God until Enoch, the seventh patriarch. 'Enoch lived sixty-five years, and begot Methuselah. After he begot Methuselah, Enoch walked with God three hundred years, and had sons and daughters… And Enoch walked with God; and he was not, for God took him.' (Genesis 5.21-24). Enoch, walking with God, was consistently close and intimate to such an extent that God shared His heart with him, as a friend. God told Enoch of the whole plan of salvation of mankind, including the flood judgement and the earthly coming of His Son, Jesus.

God showed Enoch the ultimate sacrifice, the Lamb of God, the *antitupon* of all sacrifices in the Old Testament. Jude, speaking about the patriarch Enoch, says, "Now Enoch, the seventh from Adam, prophesied about these men also, saying:

> *'Behold, the Lord comes with ten thousand of His saints to execute judgement on all, to convict all who are ungodly among them of all their ungodly deeds which they have committed in an ungodly way, and of all the harsh things which ungodly sinners have spoken against Him.'*
>
> Jude 1.14-15.

So, the earliest prophecy of the Second Coming of our Lord, Jesus Christ, came from Enoch, the seventh patriarch, about four thousand years before Jesus Christ was born. Enoch tapped far beyond his time, into our time, because he walked closely with the eternal God.

Walking so close with God would have entailed knowing the will, desires and the pleasures of God and living a life of holiness, consecration, and oneness with Him. The prophet Amos questioned, 'Can two walk together unless they are agreed?' In other words, one has to have the nature or the image of God to be able to walk with Him.

I believe Enoch literally walked with God in the garden in Eden because it was the place God had a closer relationship with Adam.

In that case, Enoch might have been given access to the Garden in Eden, either through visions, dreams and trans-locations. Therefore, Enoch might have seen God face to face or a form of His presence, but the Bible is silent about it (one can find it in extra-biblical books). The way of Access to God had been changed, after the sin of Adam. The way had to go through the sacrifice of an innocent animal. So, what special grace did Enoch have, to walk so close with God as a son of Adam? There was no 'church' and no religion. So how did he do it? There might be an ancient way which mankind is not aware of. 'Thus says the Lord; 'Stand in the ways and see, and ask for the old paths, where the good way is, and walk in it; then you will find rest for your souls.' (Jeremiah 6.16). I am interested, and would like to know the old path and pursue it.

Enoch lived at the time when sin and wickedness were dominating the world. It was the time some angels, referred to as sons of God, took wives of the daughters of men and produced sons with hybrid DNA, called mighty men and men of renown (Genesis 6.1–4).

Those hybrid sons were giants. They taught mankind wickedness, witchcraft, occultism, war, and many other evil things, so that evil and wickedness were so great on the earth that God grieved He had created mankind. God used Enoch to preach righteousness and bring correctness and repentance to the world at that time. 'By faith Enoch was taken away so that he did not see death, 'and was not found, because God had taken him', for before he was taken he had this testimony, that he pleased God.' (Hebrews 11.5). Enoch walked with God after he begot Methuselah. I believe the word of righteousness might have come to Enoch after the birth of Methuselah; how to avert the flood judgement and the final fire judgment. He heard the same Voice that walked in the Garden of Eden looking for Adam and Eve. This time, God was looking for and reaching out to the erring mankind and angels.

Enoch means 'initiated' or 'dedicated'. He was the first preacher of righteousness. He preached to the sinful world, including the fallen angels, about the coming flood judgement. His first-born son was Methuselah. The proper name 'Methuselah' means 'a man of dart' or 'a man of javelin,' but from the roots of the name – *Muth,* meaning 'death' and *'shalach'* meaning 'to bring' or 'to send forth' – the name Methuselah could mean 'his death will bring.' The Dake Annotated Reference Bible states the meaning as 'when he is dead it [the deluge] shall come.' So Enoch named Methuselah prophetically, 'his death shall bring the flood.' Methuselah lived 969 years; the longest of all the patriarchs. In the same year that Methuselah died (about 1656 years after Adam), the flood judgement came.

Enoch, as the first preacher of righteousness and repentance, was an example of "the voice of the one crying in the wilderness … make straight in the desert a highway for the Lord."

'The voice of the one crying in the wilderness; prepare the way of the Lord; make straight in the desert a highway for our God. Every valley shall be exalted and every mountain and hill brought low; the crooked places shall be made straight and the rough places smooth; the glory of the Lord shall be revealed and all flesh shall see it together … O Zion, you who brings good tidings, get up into the high mountain; O Jerusalem, you who brings good tidings, lift up your voice with strength, lift it up, be not afraid; say to the cities of Judah, 'Behold your God!' Behold the Lord God shall come with a strong hand and His arm shall rule for Him; behold His reward is with Him, and His word before Him. He will feed His flock like a shepherd; He will gather the lambs with His arm and carry them in His bosom and lead those who are with young.' Isaiah 40.3-11

Enoch brought good tidings of Jehovah's favour to the people of his day. He taught that people should lead righteous lives and change their ways so that God would have mercy on them and not bring judgement upon them. The people of his day did not listen to him.

Apostle Paul also speaks of Enoch, saying, 'Enoch was taken away so that he did not see death, and was not found, because God had taken him, for before he was taken he had this testimony that he pleased God. But without faith it is impossible to please Him, for he who comes to God must believe that He is, and that He is the rewarder of those who diligently seek Him.' (Hebrews 11.5–6). Enoch was a man of great faith and so committed himself to seeking after God, walking in faith and obedience. He brought the message of the love of God as well as the judgement of God to his generation. Enoch pleased God and was raptured/translated to heaven, without seeing death.

Enoch, the seventh patriarch, symbolises the final remnant before the great and final judgement. He points to the fact that the last perfect or matured sons of God before the Second Coming of Jesus Christ will walk with God so intimately that they will live in two realms (heaven and earth) at the same time. God will be their rest, comfort, and supply in difficult and evil times. Methuselah gave birth to Lamech and Lamech gave birth to Noah. Lamech said of Noah, 'This one will comfort us concerning our work and the toil of our hands, because of the ground which the Lord has cursed.' (Genesis 5.29).

> 'Then the Lord saw that the wickedness of man was great in the earth and that every intent of the thoughts of his heart was only evil continually. And the Lord was sorry that he had made man on the earth ... I will destroy man whom I have created from the face of the earth, both man and beast, creeping things and birds of the air, for I am sorry that I have made them, but Noah found grace in the eyes of the Lord.'
>
> Genesis 6.5-8.

Methuselah did not walk with God, nor did Lamech, son of Methuselah, but Noah was righteous and walked with God. The

Bible says, 'Noah was a just man, perfect in his generation. Noah walked with God.' (Genesis 6.9). The meaning of Noah is 'rest' or 'comfort.' He was the tenth patriarch from Adam, the second preacher of righteousness (2 Peter 2.5) and the second man who walked with God after Adam. Noah, like Enoch, lived in a terrible time; the period of time when violence, wickedness, evil, and sin were dominating the world.

The sins of Enoch's generation continued into Noah's days. As mentioned earlier, the sons of God from a previous creation sent to help mankind had married the women of the earth and had children of mixed genealogy called mighty men and men of renown:

'Now it came to pass, when men began to multiply on the face of the earth, and daughters were born to them that the sons of God saw the daughters of men, that they were beautiful; and they took wives for themselves of all whom they chose …There were giants on the earth in those days and also afterward, when the sons of God came in to the daughters of men and they bore children to them. Those were the mighty men who were of old, men of renown.' Genesis 6.1-4

The word 'giants' in Hebrew is *nephilim* (from nephil). It originates from a root word, *naphal,* meaning to fall. So, the giants could be referred to as fallen men, but they were not the same as the fallen angels who rebelled with Satan. They were living alongside mankind in the time of Adam and Eve. The mighty men and the men of renown, children of the sons of God, were people with hybrid DNA. They were half spirits and half human, and were considered as semi-gods. They had superior knowledge and ruled the humans at that time. The names of some of the giants appeared in Greek mythology as Hercules, Jupiter, Pluto, etc.

As I have mentioned above, the mighty men and the men of renown corrupted mankind and taught them fornication, adultery, evil, wickedness, war, murder, occult science, witchcraft etc.

'Wickedness of man was great in the earth and every intent of the thoughts of his heart was only evil …the earth also was corrupt before God, and the earth was filled with violence.'
Genesis 6.5, Genesis 6.11

Violence was and is one of the original characteristics of Satan. 'By the abundance of your trading you became filled with violence within, and you sinned; therefore I cast you as a profane thing, out of the mountain of God …' (Ezekiel 28.16). The world, in the time of Enoch through to Noah, was trading on the same platform as the devil, as it does today.

The root of the problem was the fact that the original human DNA was corrupted. If the activities of the mighty men and the men of renown were not stopped, the human race was doomed. 'So God looked upon the earth, and indeed it was corrupt; for all flesh had corrupted their way on the earth.' (Genesis 6.12). The devil might have intended to corrupt and destroy the seed of the woman through whom the Messiah would come. The flood judgement wiped out the mighty men and men of renown, but they found their way back to the earth and were referred to as Anak (Numbers 13.22, Joshua 15.13), Rephaims, Zumins, Emim (Genesis 14.5), Zamzummims (Deuteronomy 2.20).

'All flesh had corrupted their way on the earth' but 'Noah was a just man, perfect in his generation. Noah walked with God.' (Genesis 6.9). The Hebrew word for perfect is *tamiym*. It means complete, entire, sound, and whole. It indicated that Noah's DNA code was not corrupted or tainted. Noah had been able to separate and preserve himself from the sorcery, witchcraft, occultism and the corruption of his day. He had the perfect genetic code through which the seed of the woman (Jesus Christ) would come.

'And God said to Noah, 'The end of all flesh has come before me, for the earth is filled with violence through them; and behold I will destroy them with the earth.

Make yourself an ark of gopher-wood; make rooms in the ark, and cover it inside and outside with pitch."

Genesis 6.13-14

'By faith Noah, being divinely warned of the things not yet seen, moved with godly fear, prepared an ark for the saving of his household, by which he condemned the world and became heir of righteousness which is according to faith.'

Hebrews 11.7

Noah was warned of the flood judgement because of his walk with God. 'Things not yet seen' included 'the flood.' Scripture in Genesis 2 suggests that there had not been any rain or flood before that time, so both Enoch and Noah had no physical knowledge of the flood except for what God told them or what they might have seen spiritually. They had to take the prophecy of the flood judgement by faith. Enoch therefore was the father of faith and righteousness and Noah the heir. Enoch mentored Noah; to put it another way, the mantle of Enoch fell upon Noah. They both were teachers or preachers of righteousness and they both walked with God.

God destroyed all living creatures on earth in the flood judgement except Noah, his family and samples of each kind of all living creatures, male and female. When the flood subsided, Noah and his family came out of the ark and started the human race again. God made a rainbow covenant with Noah that He was not going to destroy the world again by flood. The new race began to multiply and build cities and nations. But mankind, left to itself without the Spirit of God, could not produce a government like that of the kingdom of heaven, so they created various imitation governmental structures and systems to govern themselves; none of them perfect. The seed of chaos and darkness through Adam was already embedded deep in mankind and man could only produce his kind.

When the Bible says that 'Noah was a just man, perfect in his generation. Noah walked with God,' it does not include Noah's wife, nor his children and their wives. Therefore, there were traces of corruption still on the face of the earth. 'And Noah begot three sons; Shem, Ham and Japheth.' Out of the three sons, Ham showed a tainted nature or DNA, the source of which might have come from the corruption of his day.

After the flood, Noah planted a vineyard, became drunk with wine and uncovered himself. His son, Ham, dishonoured his father by not covering his father's nakedness, and Noah cursed him.

> 'Cursed be Canaan; a servant of servants he shall be to his brethren ... Blessed be the Lord, the God of Shem, and may Canaan be his servant. May God enlarge Japheth and may he dwell in the tents of Shem; and may Canaan be his servants.'
> Genesis 9.26-27

God made Shem the head of his brothers and the carrier of the promised seed, family blessing, and promise, and Ham the least.

Canaan was the fourth son of Ham (Genesis 10.6). So, the curse of Ham was to be fulfilled in the life of Canaan and his descendants. The descendants of Shem would have to wait until the iniquity of the Amorites (seed of Ham) was full and ready for judgement before the blessing of Shem could be realised (Genesis 15.16).

According to the Scripture the sons of Ham were Cush (Sudanese and Ethiopians), Mizraim (Egyptians), Put (Lybians) and Canaan (Sidonians, Hittites, Jebusites, Amorites, Girgashites, Hivites, Arkites, Sinites, Arvadites, Zemarites and the Hamathites) (Genesis 10.6, 15-18). All the people who lived on the land of Canaan, which God gave to the descendants of Shem, were the descendants of Canaan. The land of Canaan was the very place the Nephilim, the mighty men and the men of renown, reappeared, so they might have been connected to the descendants of Ham.

Noah was 500 years old when he begot his three sons, Shem, Ham and Japheth (Gen 5.32). He was 600 years old when the flood came (Genesis 7.6). So, for about 100 years Noah was building the ark and preaching righteousness. The Bible indicates that the divine longsuffering waited while the ark was being prepared, but only eight people were saved from the water of judgement, the family of Noah, even though there was a Voice in the wilderness calling all the people to repentance for about 100 years (1 Peter 3.20).

Noah heard the same Voice Adam heard and Enoch heard in the garden in Eden and also became a teacher and preacher of righteousness. 'Repent, turn to the Lord. Change your ways. Change your image. Judgement is coming. The Lord is gracious, He will pardon, He will forgive if you turn to Him again.' Elijah cried in his day, 'How long will you falter between two opinions? If the Lord is God, follow Him; but if Baal follow him …' (1 Kings 18.21).

Why did the people not listen to Noah? First, the tree of the knowledge of good and evil had conditioned them to look at things around them only from the natural and the flesh's point of view. What is this old man talking about? His mind is not working properly. Everything seems alright. Why is he talking about rain and judgement?

The same attitude is still with us. Peter said, 'Knowing this first; that scoffers will come in the last days, walking according to their own lust and saying, 'Where is the promise of His coming?' For since the fathers fell asleep, all things continue as they were from the beginning of creation. For this they wilfully forget that by the word of God the heavens were of old …' (2 Peter 3.3-4).

Secondly, the people in Noah's day didn't approach the message with humility and faith. They could not believe that there would be such a rain and flood. It seemed so unnatural and unrealistic.

Thirdly, they continued with the rebellious nature of Adam. Fourthly, their culture had changed; their identity had nothing to do with God; fifth and finally, there were powerful sources, mighty men and the men of renown at the background, releasing demonic powers to enslave the people in their flesh. All these things are happening in our time.

'As it was in the days of Noah, so it will be also in the days of the son of Man. They ate, they drank, they married wives, they were given in marriage until the day that Noah entered the ark, and the flood came and destroyed them.' In the last days there will also be powerful, corrupt, demonically inspired entities, hybrids, serpentine seed or reptilian seed, who will work hard to control and enslave mankind in his flesh and sin; who will teach mankind ways of destruction and violence. Some of these entities are with us today. What do you think is the origin of the rise of sexual promiscuity, homosexuality, gay marriages, occultism, witchcraft, and abortion? All these things have been introduced demonically into our society and all of them have crept into the normal church life of today.

The ark in which Noah's family was saved was a means to their salvation and therefore a shadow of Christ. 'But of Him you are in Christ Jesus, who became for us wisdom from God – and righteousness and sanctification and redemption.' (1 Corinthians 1.30)

After the flood judgement, the first thing Noah did was to build an altar and sacrifice of the clean animals as burnt offering to the Lord. 'Then Noah built an altar to the Lord, and took of every clean animal and every clean bird, and offered burnt offerings on the altar.' (Genesis 8.20).

Each of the clean species of animals was precious and the only surviving ones on earth. Noah could have expressed his thankfulness in many ways other than sacrificing the surviving clean animals. Like Abel, Noah was righteous and acted in faith. He knew God is most holy and worthy of the best. He knew he could not please God, worship Him and have access to God any other way except through the blood sacrifice. The sacrifices of Abel and Noah were shadows of the sacrifice of Jesus Christ.

God was pleased with what Noah did. 'And the Lord smelled a soothing aroma. Then the Lord said, 'I will never again curse the ground for man's sake … nor will I again destroy every living thing as I have done.'' (Genesis 8.21-22). He blessed Noah and his household; 'Be fruitful and multiply and fill the earth.' (Genesis 9.2). Through Noah's family the world became populated again. But man, in his fallen state, continued in sin and depended on the tree of the knowledge of good and evil and not on the Spirit of God.

There was a need for a new group of people or race which will have close relationship and communion with God in order for God's purpose and will to be fulfilled on earth. God's sovereign choice fell on Abram, a descendant of Shem, to whom the promise was given. Abram was the 21st patriarch after Adam. God appeared to Abram in the pagan city of 'Ur of the Chaldees' in Mesopotamia (Genesis 11.31, Acts 7.2) and commanded him to leave his country and family to a place He would show him, and He would make him a great nation and through him all the families of the earth would be blessed (Genesis 12.1-3). Abram and family obeyed God and travelled over a thousand miles, through Haran and Damascus, to the land of Canaan.

'Brethren and fathers, listen: The God of glory appeared to our father Abraham when he was in Mesopotamia, before he dwelt in Haran, and said to him, 'Get out of your country and from your relatives, and come to a land that I will show you.' Then he came out of the land of the Chaldeans and dwelt in Haran. And from there, when his father was dead, He moved him to this land in which you now dwell.'

Acts 7.2-4

Stephen revealed that God called Abraham and gave him the promise when he was serving idols and living in the Ur of the Chaldees. Abram was to begin a new life, a new season, and birth a new godly nation through whom the divine promise, the seed of the woman who would bless the whole world, would come forth. In that completely new setting Abram had to forsake everything; his home, his family, his people, his culture and his country. He had to cut off from his past and all of its influences. He could not bring any of them into his new life.

The wife of Abram, Sarai, was barren and could not give birth to a son in Ur of the Chaldees. Ten years after the promise of God to Abram and Sarai, they were still without the promised son. When Abram complained, God told him to look at the stars. 'So shall your descendants be.' And Abram believed the Lord and He accounted it to him for righteousness" (Gen 15.5-6). Abraham walked in great faith; leaving his country and family to an un-known destination and by offering his promised son, Isaac, as a sacrifice to God (Hebrews 11.8, Hebrews 11.17). He became the father of faith both for the circumcised and the uncircumcised; the Jews, the church and the Gentiles.

However, Sarai gave her Egyptian maid to Abram, and they had a son and named him Ishmael. The Egyptians were descendants of Mizraim, the son of Ham who was cursed by Noah. Ishmael could not be part of the seed-line of the promise, who would bruise the head of the serpent. He was born out of the flesh and out of slavery (Galatians 4.21-27) and therefore could not be the lineage of the promise of Shem or the promise of the son of God. 'All the families of the earth will be blessed' and not be cursed. Ishmael was a mix-seed, and God wanted a pure seed.

God cut a covenant with Abram and said, 'Know certainly that your descendants will be strangers in a land that is not theirs, and will serve them, and they will afflict them four hundred years and also the nation whom they serve I will judge; afterwards they shall come out with great possessions.' (Genesis 15.13-15). Although God had previously spoken to Abram in visions, in Genesis 17, the Bible writes, 'When Abram was ninety-nine years old, the Lord appeared to Abram and said to him, 'I am Almighty God (El Shaddai); walk before Me and be blameless." (Genesis 17.1).

Abram was then very old, incapable of having children. Jehovah appeared to him previously, but this time God introduced Himself by a different name. He introduced Himself as El Shaddai, the All Sufficient God. 'Walk before Me and be blameless.' The Hebrew word 'before' is *paniym*. *Paniym* means 'face' or 'presence.' So, the passage can be read as 'Walk or live in my face or in my presence and be blameless.' The word blameless is the same Hebrew word, *tamiym,* translated as perfect in connection with Noah; meaning complete, entire, sound, and whole. 'Noah was a just man, perfect [*tamiym*] in his generation.' Noah did not have any corruption in his DNA or in his character as the people of his generation. After Noah, the world returned again to the heart of wickedness, evil and violence.

God needed another *tamiym* like Noah to birth a new seed-line. Abraham and his seed had to maintain a pure genetic code; unmixed with the corruption of the world. How was God going to cleanse the world from corruption if he was not going to destroy the world by the flood?

God had already prepared an answer for that contingency. 'Then Melchizedek, king of Salem brought bread and wine; he was the priest of God Most High.' (Genesis 14.18). Melchizedek was, according to Hebrews chapter seven, 'without father, without mother, without genealogy, having neither beginning of days nor end of life, but, made like the Son of God, remains a priest continually.' (Hebrews 7.3).

'Without father and mother' means Melchizedek had no Adamic issues to deal with. In other words, he did not have corrupt DNA.

Melchizedek was perfect (tamiym), like Noah. He was made like the Son of God, but He was not the Son of God. When Abram received the bread and the wine from Melchizedek, he gave him his tithe. Paul writes, 'Here mortal men receive tithes, but there he receives them, of whom it is witnessed that he lives. Even Levi, who receives tithes, paid tithes through Abraham, so to speak, for he was still in the loins of his father when Melchizedek met him.' (Heb 7.8-10).

The seed of Abraham was in his loins when he paid tithe to Melchizedek. So, the seed also paid tithe to Melchizedek and therefore shared and partook of the bread and wine from Melchizedek. The true meaning of the bread and wine which Melchizedek gave to Abraham was not revealed until Jesus Christ came. Just before He died, Jesus Christ took bread and broke it and said, 'Take, eat, this is my body.' He took the cup containing the wine and said, 'Drink from it, all of you. For this is My blood of the new covenant which is shed for the remission of sins.' (Matthew 26.26-28).

Jesus continued, 'I am the living bread which came down from heaven. If anyone eats of this bread, he will live forever; and the bread that I shall give is My flesh which I shall give for the life of the world … Unless you eat the flesh of the Son of Man and drink His blood you have no life in you. Whoever eats My flesh and drinks My blood has eternal life and I will raise him up at the last day. For My flesh is food indeed and My blood is drink indeed.' (John 6.51-56).

The Bible says, 'Many of His disciples, when they heard this said, 'This is a hard saying, who can understand it?' Who could eat the flesh and drink the blood of humans except idol worshippers? However, Jesus Christ was referring to His perfect DNA which He carried in His body and blood. The Word was implanted into the womb of the mother of Jesus, Mary, when the Holy Spirit overshadowed her. Jesus also did not have an earthly father or seed but God's seed. He was and is without sin and had a perfect DNA, like the first Adam before his fall (Hebrews 4.15). Abraham and his seed shall partake of the perfect image and likeness of God through Jesus Christ. That was the power in the bread and the wine which Melchizedek gave to Abraham. The understanding of which was far beyond Abram's time and stretched into our time. 'Your father Abraham rejoiced to see My day, and he saw it and was glad.' (John 8.56, Rom 8.29).

Through Abraham a pure DNA code was maintained and transferred to his seed. 'Now to Abraham and his Seed were the promises made.' He does not say, 'And to Seeds,' as of many, but as of one, 'And to your Seed,' who is Christ (Galatians 3.16). Jesus Christ on the earth inherited the promise of Abraham, and through Him all the families of the earth will be saved.

We are the seed of Abraham through Christ and therefore we must also maintain a pure DNA, walk before God and be blameless to inherit the promise; 'And if you are Christ's, then you are Abraham's seed, and heirs according to the promise.' (Galatians 3.29). Abraham 'waited for the city which has foundation, whose builder and maker is God.' That city was heaven. Those who would inherit heaven must walk blameless before God, perfect and pure without any DNA corruption. This is an eternal message to the church of today.

Enoch and Noah walked with *Elohim*, but Abraham walked before *El Shaddai*. Just as Noah and his seed were saved from the flood judgement, so Abraham and his seed will be saved from future judgements if they walked in God's face (*tamiym*) blameless. 'Just as He chose us in Him before the foundation of the world, that we should be holy and without blame before Him in love, having predestined us to adoption as sons by Jesus Christ to Himself according to the good pleasure of His will.' (Ephesians 1.4-5).

God told Abram, 'And I will make My covenant between Me and you and will multiply you exceedingly ... My covenant is with you, and you shall be a father of many nations. No longer shall your name be called Abram, but your name shall be Abraham; for I have made you a father of many nations … As for Sarai your wife, you shall not call her name Sarai, but Sarah shall be her name. And I will bless her, and she shall be a mother of nations; kings of people shall be from her.' (Genesis 17.2-16). The Lord, the I AM, breathed Himself into their names and changed their names; from Abram to Abraham and from Sarai to Sarah. Abraham means 'father of many nations' and Sarah means 'mother of nations.' The change of names was very important because it gave them new identities; earthly people with changed DNA.

God waited for the time both Abraham and Sarah were incapable of having children because the seed was to be a promised seed, of faith, supernatural and not of the natural. Both Abraham and Sarah thought that Ishmael was going to fulfil the promise. But God said, 'No, Sarah your wife shall bear a son, and you shall call his name Isaac; I will establish my covenant with him for an everlasting covenant, and with his descendants after him.' (Genesis 17.19). Isaac must be the son of Abraham and not the son of Abram.

'By faith Sarah herself also received strength to conceive seed, and she bore a child when she was past the age, because she judged Him faithful who had promised. Therefore from one man, and him as good as dead, were born as many as the stars of the sky in multitude – innumerable as the sand which is by the seashore.' (Hebrews 11.11-12). Isaac, the promised son born out of faith, was like a resurrection son, a type of Christ. Unlike Ishmael, the seed of Isaac came through the circumcision (cutting of the foreskin) of Abraham.

Scripture says that Abraham believed God and it was accounted to him for righteousness. And he was called the friend of God (James 2.23, 2 Chronicles 20.7). God Himself called Abraham His friend (Isaiah 41.08). It means Abraham did not just walk in

God presence, but he also walked with God as a friend. In other words, Abraham had a very close relationship and fellowship with *El Shaddai*, just as Enoch and Noah had with *Elohim*.

God Himself said, 'Shall I hide from Abraham what I am doing …?' Abraham interceded on behalf of Sodom and Gomorrah as a friend of God and also as a priest. Abraham, like Enoch, received the revelation of God's plan of salvation for mankind through Jesus Christ. Jesus told the Jews, 'Your father Abraham rejoiced to see My day, and he saw it and was glad.' (John 8.56). Therefore, Abraham like Enoch and Noah lived beyond his time. As a friend of God, Abraham might have seen God's face, but was silent about it.

Of the three patriarchs Enoch, Noah and Abraham, who were perfect and walked with God, it was only Abraham with whom God made an everlasting covenant which included his seed. 'This is my covenant which you shall keep, between Me and you and your descendants [seed] after you: Every male child among you shall be circumcised; and you shall be circumcised in the flesh of your foreskins, and it shall be a sign of the covenant between Me and you.' (Genesis 17.11)

The Hebrew word for sign is *'owth'* (oth). It means signal, flag, beacon, mark, standard, memorial, omen, and symbol. For Noah and the future generation, the sign was a rainbow. It showed the mercy and the love of God to mankind at the same time pointing to something new; a new way of dealing with corruption. For Abraham and his seed, the sign of the covenant was circumcision.

Circumcision was a pointer to a new way of holiness and to their destiny as a kingdom of priests and a holy nation. Every seed of this nation must pass through circumcision. Why? It is a sign of not walking in the flesh but walking in the Spirit. 'To be carnally minded is death; but to be spiritually minded is life and peace … they that are in the flesh cannot please God.' (Romans 8.6-8).

The Bible says **Abraham** was ninety-nine years old when he was circumcised in the flesh of his foreskin. It was possible that other nations were practising some form of circumcision. But God said, 'He who is eight days old among you shall be circumcised, every male child in your generation …' 'Then Abraham circumcised his son Isaac when he was eight days old, as God had commanded him.' (Gen 17.12, Gen 21.4).

Why the eighth day? Science has proven that in a newly born child the blood has no clotting ability. Therefore, any form of bleeding may prove fatal. In modern times the medics may give vitamin K to a new-born child to initiate production of the blood coagulating protein, called prothrombin. In the 20th century, it was scientifically acknowledged that prothrombin is at its highest level, throughout the life of the person, on the eighth day. So, God, as the **Creator**, was way ahead of modern science.

Circumcision involved the cutting off of the foreskin of the male genital organ. It is the sign or the mark of separation of the heart from the things of the flesh and the world (Romans 2.28-29). It was the sign that they were *tamiym,* just as God had told their father Abraham, a sign that they were God's people. The seed of Abraham would cast a shadow on the earth, or become God's image on earth, through whom the whole world would be blessed and be reconciled to God.

The covenant with Abraham also included the Promised Land, which was a picture of heaven. 'Lift your eyes now and look from the place where you are − northward, southward, eastward and westward; for all the land which you see I give to you and your descendants forever.' (Genesis 13.14-15). Bible says the Lord appeared to Isaac, the son of Abraham, when he decided to go to Egypt in the time of famine, saying, 'Do not go to Egypt; live in the land of which I shall tell you. Dwell in this land and I will be with you and bless you; for to you and your descendants I give all these lands and I will perform the oath which I swore to Abraham your father. And I will make your descendants multiply as the stars of heaven; I will give to your descendants all these lands; in your seed all the nations of the earth shall be blessed because Abraham obeyed My voice and kept my charge, My commandments, My statutes and My laws.' (Genesis 26.2-5).

Before the Mosaic Law was enacted, Abraham knew about the charge of the Lord, the commandments, the statutes, and the law, and kept them to the pleasure of God. So, the commandments, the statutes and the law could be seen as a shadow of God's own image. In them God revealed His nature. The blessing of Isaac, Jacob and the children of Israel was due to the sacrifice of one man, Abraham. 'Now to Abraham and his Seed were the promises made. He does not say, 'And to seeds, as of many, but as of one, 'And to your Seed', who is Christ.' (Galatians 3.16). So, through the Seed, Jesus Christ, the Seed of the woman, the whole family of the earth is blessed.

The Bible does not mention in what form *El Shaddai* appeared to Abraham. The same God appeared to Isaac and introduced Him, 'I am the God of your father Abraham, do not fear, for I am with you. I will bless you and multiply your descendants for My servant Abraham's sake.' (Genesis 26.24). Again, the Bible does not tell us in what form *El Shaddai* appeared to Isaac.

Isaac also begot twins, Esau and Jacob. Esau was the elder, but it was Jacob who by divine choice carried the seed of promise. Jacob gave birth to 12 sons and those sons became the fathers of the twelve tribes of Israel. The same God, *El Shaddai*, appeared to Jacob as he fled from his brother Esau.

'So he came to a certain place and stayed there all night, because the sun had set. And he took one of the stones of that place and put it at his head, and he lay down in that place to sleep. Then he dreamed, and behold, a ladder was set up on earth, and its top reached to heaven; and there the angels of God were ascending and descending on it. And behold, the Lord stood above it and said; "I am the Lord

Jacob perceived, 'This is none other than the house of God, and this is the gate of heaven.' (Gen 28.17). He called the place Bethel, the house of God. Here again the Abrahamic covenant was confirmed and renewed in Jacob. The same promise given to Abraham applied to Isaac and Jacob. When Jacob returned to Bethel, after 20 years in exile, God told him to build an altar to the God who appeared to him when he fled from Esau, his brother. 'And he (Jacob) built an altar there and called the place El Bethel (God of the house of God) because there God appeared to him when he fled from the face of his brother.' (Genesis 35.7).

The Hebrew word for 'appeared' used in Genesis 35 verse 7 is *'galah,'* meaning to uncover, unveil and to reveal. The word suggests the idea of the exposure of one's nakedness. So, at Bethel, God uncovered Himself to Jacob. In other words, God revealed a mystery about Himself. First, there was a gulf, a chasm between the earth and the heaven. Secondly, the chasm was bridged by a ladder or staircase on which one could ascend step by step to God. Third, angels were ascending and descending on the staircase. Fourth, God stood at the top of the staircase.

The earth can be seen as representing man. Man is essentially dust, earth. There was a gulf separating man and God and His kingdom. Jesus, referring to Jacob's revelation, said that, 'hereafter you shall see heaven open, and the angels of God ascending and descending upon the Son of Man.' (John 1.51). Jesus therefore solved the mystery of the nakedness of God; that He, Jesus Christ, was the staircase Jacob saw in his dream. In other words, nobody can see who God really is except through Jesus Christ. When God uncovers Himself, He reveals Jesus Christ, the brightness of His glory and the express image of His person. The angels are the ministering spirits sent forth to minister the grace and love of God on earth (Hebrews 1.14).

Jacob stayed at the place of revelation all night because the sun had set. 'The sun had set' may refer to the last days or the end times. In the end times God will uncover Himself and reveal Jesus Christ in a special way that His people might have greater access to the King and His kingdom. In the end times angelic ministry will increase and people will live under open heaven.

God, in El Bethel, confirmed the change of name He had earlier effected in Jacob. 'Your name is Jacob; your name shall not be called Jacob anymore, but Israel shall be your name.' (Genesis 35.10). Jacob means 'heel catcher, supplanter' and Israel means 'he who wrestles with God' or 'Prince of God.' So Jacob's identity was also changed to reflect his assignment. 'Your name shall no longer be called Jacob, but Israel; for you have struggled with God and with men and have prevailed.' (Genesis 32.28). The MKJV version says, 'For like a prince you have power with God and with men.' Israel as a prince of God shall prevail in prayer with God and over all its enemies on earth.

Looking prophetically at Enoch, Noah, and Jacob in the reverse order, Jacob represents a sinful generation, needing a Mediator, Jesus Christ, between it and heaven; Noah represents the righteous saved by the grace of Jesus Christ; by the ark or the wood of His death; while Enoch represents the cleansed, matured and prepared bride of Jesus Christ. In Enoch we see the catching up of the saints, when the church had not yet been born. Amazing!

Mankind has to go full circle. 'As it was at the beginning, so shall it be at the end.' We shall be like the first Adam before his fall. This is God who declares the end from the beginning and from ancient times things that are not yet done (Isaiah 46.10). There was a Voice of God which walked in the garden in Eden when Adam sinned. The same Voice came to Enoch, to Noah, to Abraham, to Isaac, to Jacob, to Moses, and to other power-ful prophets like Elijah, Isaiah, etc. until finally, the Word, Jesus Christ became flesh. The same Voice continues as the Voice in the wilderness calling people to repentance and return to the kingdom. 'Repent, the kingdom of God is at hand.'

CHAPTER 2

The Voice In The Fire

According to the word of God, 70 people of the seed of Abraham, in the time of Joseph, the governor of Egypt, went to live in Egypt for over 200 years. God's promise of multiplication of the seed of Abraham began to be seen in Egypt. The children of Israel grew greatly in number (Genesis 47.27). A new Egyptian Pharaoh arose who saw the children of Israel as a threat. 'Look, the children of Israel are more and mightier than we; come, let us deal shrewdly with them …' (Exodus 1.9-10).

Egypt enacted new laws and set taskmasters over the children of Israel, to afflict, maltreat and force them into hard and bitter bondage. It was to break the spirit of the children of Israel, bring them under reproach, rob them of their freedom, ruin their health, shorten their lives and decrease their number. The bondage also affected the relationship between the children of Israel and their Hebrew God and introduced them to the worship of Egyptian idols and gods. Therefore, the culture and worldview of the children of Israel were altered, but the children of Israel continued to multiply, even under that oppression, because of their covenant with God through Abraham.

God told Abraham that he would be a father of many nations and that his seed would be strangers in a land and be afflicted for four hundred years. 'And also the nation whom they serve I will judge; afterward they shall come out with great possessions.' (Genesis 17.4, Genesis 15.13-14) When the time of their freedom came and a deliverer was to be born, Pharaoh issued another law, that all new-born sons of the children of Israel should be sacrificed to the Nile god. It was in that period that Moses was born.

I believe the devil, through Pharaoh, was trying to stop the deliverer of the children of Israel. It happened again under King Herod, who ruled over the Jews, when Jesus was born. King Herod killed all the male children aged two years and under in Bethlehem and all its districts in order to eliminate the Messiah (Matthew 2.16). But he was unsuccessful.

Moses was therefore born of Israelite slaves in Egypt but was adopted by the 'daughter of Pharaoh' (Exodus 2.25) and lived as a prince in Egypt. Stephen, in Acts 7.22, says, 'And Moses was learned in all the wisdom of the Egyptians and was mighty in words and deeds.' Moses looked to all people as an Egyptian but in his heart, like all the children of Abraham, burned flickers of the light of a covenant with El Shaddai, the God of Abraham. Moses tried to set free an Israelite by killing an Egyptian when the two were engaged in a fight. When the matter became known to Pharaoh, Moses fled from Egypt in fear of his life and settled in Midian as an ordinary shepherd.

After forty years of silent work as a shepherd in Midian, Moses had become a family man, with a wife named Zipporah, the daughter of his master Jethro, and two sons, Gershom and Eliezer. He had settled down to the life of a shepherd. Tending a flock was now his proper profession. At the age of 80, he might have forgotten about his people in bondage and established himself comfortably with his new occupation and his new family. But one day, as Moses tended the flock of his father-in-law, he came to Horeb, the mountain of God (also called Mount Sinai). He was doing his normal and daily work.

> *'And the Angel of the Lord appeared to him in a flame of fire from the midst of the bush so he looked, and behold, the bush was burning with fire, but the bush was not consumed.'*
>
> Exodus 3.2

The Hebrew word for 'Lord' is Jehovah. It is one of the names of the revelation of God, meaning Self-Existing One. Angels are spiritual beings who serve in the government of Jehovah on many and varied levels and duties. I do not believe the angel of the Lord refers to pre-incarnated Jesus. The Hebrew word for angel is *malak* and it means one dispatched as a deputy; a messenger and ambassador. The angel of the Lord is special to Him. He is not only a messenger but an ambassador and a herald of Jehovah. So, many times the angel would speak like Jehovah and open the door for Jehovah to interact with mankind. In this book the Lord and Jehovah will be used interchangeably.

Moses had seen countless numbers of bush fires but the one in question fascinated him. With all his education and experiences in Egypt and in the desert, Moses had never seen such a phenomenon before. The fire was burning but the bush was not consumed. The fire therefore was self-existing and seemed not to depend on the bush or any external source for energy. Impossible! Where did it get its energy from? Moses said, 'I will now turn aside and see this great sight, why the bush does not burn.'

> *'So when the Lord saw that he turned aside to look, God called to him from the midst of the bush, and said, 'Moses, Moses!' and he said, 'Here I am."*
>
> Exodus 3.4

Moses did not just pass by or ignore the strange sight. When Moses turned to investigate the matter, God then had his attention, so He called his personal name, Moses, Moses. God called him who was seeking, whose attention was turned towards seeking the truth. Many of us, right from our childhood through school, through the media and our culture, have been programmed out of the knowledge and faith in God. We approach the Bible with a secular cultural mind-set and sometimes with a theological or religious bias. Are we really prepared for the truth? Can we handle the truth?

Moses realised that the fire was not only strange but alive. The fire had a voice. It can talk in a language he could understand. And it knew his name. God began to warn Moses.

'Do not draw near this place, take your sandals off your feet, for the place where you stand is holy ground.'

Exodus 3.5

Oh my God! The fire was not just living but holy as well. For a long time, over two hundred years since the children of Israel lived in Egypt, God had not manifested Himself to anyone, but in the time of Moses He manifested Himself to Moses as a flame of fire and began to draw the parameters of their relationship. For the first time we have an idea how God manifests Himself. Fire!

1. Do not draw near this place.
2. Take the sandals off your feet.
3. The place where you stand is holy ground.

There are always parameters when it comes to a communion with someone superior, more so with the supreme God. Let us take a cursory look at these parameters.

Do Not Draw Near This Place

'Do not draw near this place…' was a command and a warning. Moses saw the flame of fire and was stopped getting closer for his own good. He would have come under God's immediate judgement and possibly might have been burnt alive. It gave Moses the chance to have an appreciation of who he was, where he was and whom he was communicating with. The restriction drew a boundary and set up limits between God and Moses. No one is righteous before God, and no one is holy like the Lord (Romans 3.10, 1 Samuel 2.2). Therefore, Moses was deemed unholy before God, and needed to be sanctified first.

Moses told the children of Israel later, 'For the Lord our God is a consuming fire, a jealous God.' (Deuteronomy 4.24). Apostle Paul also describes God as 'He who is the blessed and only Potentate, the King of kings and Lord of lords, who alone has immortality, dwelling in unapproachable light which no man has seen or can see …' 'For our God is a consuming fire.' (1 Timothy 6.15-16, Hebrews 12.29). God is a consuming fire, a Jealous God and dwells in unapproachable Light. He will consume anyone before Him who is unholy.

Take The Sandals Off Your Feet

The obvious physical reason why it was necessary for Moses to take off his sandals was that there was dust on them, so Moses would have trampled upon the place with dust and made it dirty. Spiritually, it meant his walk or life was unclean. To keep the sandals on would have meant spiritually defiling the place. Taking the sandals off symbolically removed the uncleanness and the unholiness. In another episode, the Commander of the Lord's army said to Joshua, 'Take the sandal off your foot, for the place where you stand is holy.' (Joshua 5.15). Therefore, the main reason for removing the sandals was because the place he was standing was holy and was not to be defiled.

Secondly, a sandal is a sign of authority and taking it off indicates the surrender of one's authority. In the story of Ruth in the Bible, the close relative of Boaz removed his sandals because he decided not to redeem the estate of Naomi which fell to him (Ruth 4.8). Therefore, his honour or authority was taken from him and given to Boaz, who was next in line to redeem the family estate. Moses took off his honour and authority before God when he took off his sandals. It was a sign of humility and surrender before God.

Thirdly, it was the sign of honour and respect to God and to the place where God had manifested His presence. It was and is the practice in the Middle East, including Egypt, to take off the sandals when one went to temples and holy places. Before the true and holy God Moses was not expected to keep his sandals on.

The Place where You Stand Is Holy

Every place God reveals Himself becomes holy. The patriarchs would build altars to mark such places and to consecrate them. At the time God called Moses, he had not been sanctified or consecrated. In other words, he was unholy. However, the fact that the tree was not consumed meant that God's holiness had overshadowed the tree and the place. To see the fire of God is one thing but to enter into it is quite another thing altogether; they are not the same. Moses would later be invited to enter the fire of God, but at that first encounter he was not invited because he was deemed unholy. This suggests a process of transformation or sanctification.

If we want to know God, before we can 'party' with Him, perhaps the first thing we should know and understand is, 'God is holy'. God is the source of all holiness. Holiness is God's nature. It is the very essence of His being; His invisible, proper, and essential nature, that which makes Him who He is. If His holiness is breached, God will no longer be God. Modern Christianity has reduced God only to a 'good natured benevolent person' upstairs whose purpose is to attend to and supply her needs and wants. We have come to approach God as if He is just anybody, sometimes with such disrespect. No! The God of the Bible is a holy God. And there is none holy like Him.

Psalmist says, 'Exalt the Lord our God, and worship at His holy hill; for the Lord our God is holy.' (Psalms 99.9). Not only is God holy but He alone is holy as Scriptures reveal. 'No one is holy like the Lord, for there is none besides You, nor is there any rock like our God.' (1 Samuel 2.2). The victorious saints sung in Revelations 15, 'Who shall not fear You, O Lord, and glorify Your name? For You alone are holy …' (Revelations 15.4).

Speaking through prophet Isaiah, God said, 'And there is no other God besides Me, a just and a Saviour; there is none besides me.'

(Isaiah 45.21b). In Isaiah 46.9-10 God says, 'Remember the former things of old, for I am God, and there is no other; I am God and there is none like Me. Declaring the end from the beginning, and from ancient times things that are not yet done.' (Isaiah 46.9-10). God's holiness, therefore, separates Him from man, angels, anyone or anything in the universe whether living or not.

The common Hebrew words used for holy are *'qados'*, meaning separated or set apart and *'qodesh'*, meaning separateness or apartness. When used of God, it refers to God's absolute separateness, uniqueness, and distinctness over and above everyone and everything in all things. He cannot be touched or be influenced by sin, evil, death, space, or time. He cannot be mixed with anything. God is therefore absolute pure and perfection in word and deed. No one therefore can be in God's dimension and know Him and describe Him unless he reveals Himself.

As a flame of fire, God has infinite ability to judge, cleanse, purify, expose, empower, consume or destroy as the physical copy of spiritual fire and light. Moses later warned the children of Israel that the Lord God is a consuming fire, a jealous God (Deuteronomy 4.24). The Fire of God is jealous. It will consume everything that is unholy before it, including man but it will not consume anything declared holy. He is the sole object of our love and worship and will judge and consume any idolatry, sin, or rebellion.

When Moses obeyed God and removed his sandals, God continued to speak to him and put him in line with the promises and the covenants He made to Abraham and his seed.

'Moreover He said, 'I am the God of your father – the God of Abraham, the God of Isaac and the God of Jacob.' And Moses hid his face, for he was afraid to look upon Him.'
Exodus 3.6

God did not say, 'I was,' but 'I am' the God of your father. Even though Abraham, Isaac and Jacob were dead, hundreds of years ago, they were still alive, and God was still their God. It meant Abraham, Isaac and Jacob found the city they were waiting for, the heavenly city (Hebrews 11.10). Jesus Christ referred to this passage and said that "God is not the God of the dead but of the living." (Matthew 22.32). God also did not say 'your fathers' but 'your father,' referring directly to Abraham. So Moses was going to inherit or walk in the promises of Abraham, even though Moses was the seventh generation after Abraham.

It might have been a startling revelation to Moses. The very God whom my forefathers believed and worshipped is a living God? God had fulfilled His heavenly promises to Abraham, Isaac, and Jacob in such a way that even though they were physically dead, they were still alive. It meant the covenants and the promises made to them were also alive. God had not forgotten His covenants and His promises made to them over hundreds of years ago. Therefore, God is a living God, a faithful God and will fulfil His promises to the children of Israel, the seed of Abraham. The words of God might have warmed Moses' heart and strengthened him. But it might also have brought the fear of God into his heart. He was face to face with the living God and therefore was afraid to look upon Him.

> 'And the Lord said: 'I have surely seen the oppression of My people who are in Egypt, and have heard their cry because of their taskmasters, for I know their sorrows. So I have come down to deliver them out of the hand of the Egyptians, and bring them up from that land to a good and large land, to a land flowing with milk and honey, to the place of the Canaanites, and the Hittites and the Amorites and the Perizzites and the Hivites and the Jebusites.'"
>
> Exodus 3.7-8

Adam heard the Voice of God in the garden in Eden; Jacob saw God and heard His voice on top of a ladder in a dream; but Moses heard the Voice of God in the wilderness. God Himself came down to the earth and appeared in a flame of fire to deliver His people.

God told Abram that his children would be strangers in a land and be afflicted four hundred years (Genesis 15.13). Abram received the promise when he was 75 years old. 25 years later he gave birth to Isaac. 5 years latter Isaac was weaned and scoffed off by Ishmael, so Ishmael and Hagar were sent away. Isaac was 60 when he begot Jacob (Gen 25.26) and Jacob was 130 when he went to Egypt (Genesis 47.9). It means that for 190 years (60+130) the children of Israel were not living in Egypt. However, the affliction of Isaac started 5 years after Isaac was born. This brings down the number to 185 years. So, the children of Israel might have lived 215 years (400–185) in Egypt.

The Bible also says, 'Now the sojourn of the children of Israel who lived in Egypt was four hundred and thirty years. And it came to pass at the end of the four hundred and thirty years – on that very same day – it came to pass that all the armies of the Lord went out from the land of Egypt.' (Exodus 12.40-41). If we include Abraham's life in Israel until Isaac was weaned (25+5), they lived as strangers in a foreign land for 430 years.

As an eternal God, He knew that the oppression and the affliction of the children of Israel would be very great and severe in Egypt at the time when the sin of the Amorites was full. God promised he would deliver them at the end of 400 years. The time had come. God said, 'So I have come down to deliver them out of the hand of the Egyptians.' Jehovah came down Himself. His physical presence was on earth to deliver the children of Israel and fulfil His promise. There was no other way for the children of Israel to be free from Egypt.

Moses was seeing the flame of fire as God's physical and/or manifest presence and not His attribute. God was the Deliverer and the Redeemer. 'As for our Redeemer, the Lord of hosts is His name, the Holy One of Israel.' (Isaiah 47.4). God was about to deliver the children of Israel from Egypt and lead them to the promised land, a large land, flowing with milk and honey; from the place of slavery and bondage to a place of freedom, from a place of lack to a place of plenty, from one place to another. God will not deliver you into a vacuum. God already had a place prepared for them. You must be aware that God has a place prepared for you.

Exodus 3.9

God had surely seen the oppression of His people in Egypt and His compassion was stirred (Exodus 3.7). What about Moses, the caring shepherd? Did he also see the suffering of the children of Israel after living forty years in Midian as a shepherd? "Behold, the cry of the children of Israel has come to Me." God was emphasizing the point, driving it home into the heart of Moses. Moses was supposed to see what God was seeing at that time, the current perception of God, not 40 years ago. God wanted Moses as a caring shepherd to see it again, from His perspective, to have His heart and His divine compassion. Moses freed an Israelite 40 years ago, but it was not God's timing. He must now walk in God's timing, according to the good pleasure of His will, which He purposed in Himself (Ephesians 1.5; 9).

Exodus 3.9-10

God was the Redeemer and the Deliverer, but He needed a representative, an ambassador on the earthly realm. 'The earth God has given to the children of men.' Moses was being appointed and sent to deliver the children of Israel from slavery and bring them out of Egypt through the influence and power of God. The Voice in the garden looking for Adam, His friend, had become the Voice in the wilderness looking to redeem His covenant people, Israel. Moses was being commissioned a prophet of God; the one carrying the Voice in the wilderness. He was being made a type of the New Testament apostle and a type of the Great Apostle, Jesus Christ, the Messiah and the Redeemer.

Throughout the 40 years as a servant and a shepherd, Moses did not know that God was preparing him. Anybody who is sent carries the power and the authority of him who sent him. God requires first a servant's heart, and an obedient heart. 'Jesus made Himself of no reputation, taking the form of a bondservant and came in the likeness of men …' 'Though He was a Son, yet He learned obedience by the things which He suffered.'

If one cannot be a servant then one cannot serve God. The Centurion answered Jesus, 'For I also am a man under authority, having soldiers under me. And I say to one, 'Go,' and he goes; and to another, 'Come,' and he comes; and to my servant, 'Do this,' and he does it." Without placing oneself under authority, one does not have authority to act and to serve.

Today's church is full of leaders who have not first learnt to serve. Everything is geared towards their own ends; their exaltation and recognition. They have to be served. 'For even the Son of God did not come to be served, but to serve, and to give His life a ransom for many.' It is only when we serve that we begin to understand the heart of God. No, God will not send you until you are ready. The iron will be in the fire until it is red hot. Then it is moulded to match the designer plan. Yes, the world will hear you, and acknowledge you when God first certifies you. 'This is My Beloved Son in whom I am well pleased. Hear Him!'

There is so much competition among the Pastors today that we have lost the fact that we have the same mission and are serving the same God. Even churches and Pastors want and pray for other churches and Pastors to go down and to be in trouble so that they can be seen to be better than others. They forget that they are working against God. Envy, jealousy, and pride have filled many of us Pastors, Prophets, and Apostles. If God begins to lift up a Pastor or any man or woman of God, the first opposition and attack would come from fellow Pastors, fellow ministers of God and fellow Christians.

We have covered our envy, jealousy and pride so nicely and carefully that we deceive ourselves that we don't have them. We have a nice veneer but the inside is rotten; whitewashed sepulchres. The disobedient, the rebellious and the stubborn cannot truthfully serve under others; they only work to serve themselves. Even when they are under senior ministers, they are still serving themselves. They are wolves in sheep clothing. These people pretend they are serving God, but they cannot serve under anybody, not even God; they serve themselves. They compete with God for the glory. They want the glory for themselves. The devil did the same thing and was thrown down from heaven.

'God is Light and there is no darkness in Him at all … But if we walk in the light as He is in the light, we have fellowship with one another, and the blood of Jesus Christ, His Son cleanses us from all sin.' You see, we take this metaphorically and see light as referring to goodness, excellence, purity, truth, knowledge, wisdom, and happiness, which is true. But the true fact is that God is literally Light, and so you must walk in this literal light of God. The question is do you walk in the invisible Light of God? What sort of light are you walking in? What lamp is under your feet? What light lightens your path? Many of us are not walking in the true Light of God even though we pretend we are? Sometimes half-light or half-truth is more dangerous and more deceptive than darkness.

The I AM

Moses had had a live encounter with the living God, and he was in the process of being sent to go back to Egypt to redeem the children of Israel from slavery and hard bondage. Moses had lived in Egypt before. He knew the might of Pharaoh and the power of the Egyptian army. Egypt was the most powerful nation at that time. God did not offer Moses any army or any special weapon to use, so he rightly questioned his own identity: 'Who am I that I should go to Pharaoh, and that I should bring the children of Israel out of Egypt?' In other words, 'I am just an ordinary shepherd.' 'I am nobody before Pharaoh; the greatest king in the world, and His army.' 'You need a more powerful army and an army general, not me.'

God's answer to Moses' question was, 'I will certainly be with you. And this shall be a sign to you that I have sent you. When you have brought the people out of Egypt, you shall serve God on this mountain.' (Exodus 3.12).

If Moses understood it right, God was saying that His presence was more powerful and more potent than Pharaoh and the Egyptian army. He might have been even more bewildered. Well! Moses said, 'Indeed, when I come to the children of Israel and say to them, 'The God of your fathers has sent me to you,' and they say to me, 'What is His name?' What shall I say to them?' The name of God is the epitome of who He is; what He carries, His authority and power. So Moses was asking, 'Who are you? Which type of God are you? What power and authority do you have and carry?' In other words, 'In what power and authority are You sending me?' Moses was asking, not only for the children of Israel but also for Himself.

> *'I AM WHO I AM. And He said, 'Thus you shall say to the children of Israel, 'I AM has sent me to you.'*
>
> Exodus 3.14

Who is I AM? The Hebrew word translated as I AM is '*hayah*', which means 'to exist', 'to be', 'to become' or 'to come to pass'. In other words, He is the life of everything. Everything exists because He Is. He is the being of everything without Him nothing is. He is timeless and the source of everything. I AM is thus a self-existing and self-sufficient God, He does not need man, animal, or anything in order to exist; rather, He is a life giver. That was the God of the burning bush. He did not need the bush to exist; completely self-existing and self-sufficient. He is the source, beginning and the end of everything. God signalled that 'I AM' was to be His proper and personal name.

The Hebrew word, *Jehovah / Yahweh* translated as 'Lord,' is derived from the same Hebrew word, *'hayah'* meaning self-existing and self-sufficient God. According to Jewish tradition, the name Jehovah/Yahweh was too holy to be mentioned, so it was usually written without the vowels as YHWH (Tetragrammaton). The children of Israel instead would use the word *Adonai* as a substitute of Jehovah/Yahweh (Genesis 18.3).

Jehovah is a God of intimacy who seeks and encourages a closer intimacy with Him. Jehovah God breathed Himself into Adam and Adam became a living being. Adam therefore had God's DNA or nature inside of him. Jehovah God was one with Adam before his fall. Jehovah God put Adam in the garden in Eden and endowed him with glory, honour, and dominion (Psalms 8.5-8). So there was a natural affinity and bonding between Jehovah God and Adam, to such an extent that Jehovah God used to visit Adam and Eve in the garden. In whatever way one sees it, relationship, love, friendship, intimacy, or sonship, there was a close bond between Jehovah God and man.

> *'Moreover God said to Moses, 'Thus you shall say to the children of Israel; The Lord God of your fathers, the God of Abraham, the God of Isaac, and the God of Jacob, has sent me to you. This is My name forever, and this is My memorial to all generation.''*
>
> Exodus 3.15

God later revealed to Moses saying, 'I am Lord (Jehovah), I appeared to Abraham, to Isaac, and to Jacob as God Almighty (El Shaddai), but by My name Lord (Jehovah)! I was not known to them. I have also established My covenant with them, to give them the land of Canaan, the land of their pilgrimage, in which they were strangers.' (Exodus 6.2-4).

When Adam and Eve sinned and lost their communion with God, it was *Jehovah Elohim* who sought them, killed innocent animals, and clothed them with the tunics (Genesis 3.21). Though Adam and Eve lost their intimacy with God, Jehovah did not abandon them. He chastised them for their sin, but He also sought to redeem them from the mess they had put themselves in. He is still Jehovah God to us; sorting out our mess. God has revealed the attributes of the name Jehovah in many ways, but the first distinct revelation of the name *Jehovah* was in connection with the redemption of Israel. Therefore I AM (Jehovah) is a powerful redemptive name of God.

Through the revelation of the name Jehovah, God began to unfold a personal relationship and communion with man, not only His works but His manifest presence. Mankind through God's dealing with Moses and the children of Israel began to know who God was personally, His nature and His character. In that relationship Jehovah had to deal with three things:

1. His holiness in relation to man's sinfulness (Leviticus 11.44-45; 19.1-2; 20.26; Habakkuk 1.12-13).
2. His response to sin (Genesis 6.5-7; Exodus 34.6-7; Deuteronomy 32.35-42; Psalms 11.4-6; 66.18).
3. His love for the righteous redemption of sinners (Genesis 3.2; 8.20-21; Leviticus 16.2-3; Isaiah 53.5-10).

Jehovah is the God who manifests His Presence; "My presence will go with you." He is the God of signs and wonders, as He demonstrated to Moses and all Israel. Jehovah is the God of love, mercy, compassion, and grace. The manifest presence of God also manifests His attributes, who He is, and opens up the resources of heaven,

Apostle Paul ended Hebrews chapter 11 with these words, 'And all these (men of faith) having obtained a good testimony through faith, did not receive the promise. God having provided something better for us that they should not be made perfect apart from us.' (Hebrews 11.39-40). Of all the mighty works the patriarchs and mighty men of old did, they did not receive the complete promise. The word 'perfect' means completeness and wholeness as we have seen. It shows that God planned that the mighty men of faith and the prophets of old should not complete their works but wait for us, in the end time, to join hands together with us to complete their works.

God will therefore release their mantles upon us and/or send them here on earth to encourage, strengthen, direct, guide and empower us to fulfil the complete plan of redemption and restoration. They have a share in it. They sacrificed so much for it. We have many examples of this in the Bible. One clear example is when Moses and Elijah appeared to Jesus at the transfiguration and spoke to Him about His death on the cross. Why? Couldn't God have strengthened Jesus Himself? It was God's administrative style and His governmental process. It was God's will and pleasure. The eleventh-hour saints shall receive as much as the first-hour saints. It is still His will and His pleasure. No one can do anything about it. It is not only Elijah who will come back again before the coming of the Lord, but Moses too will come back again in one way or the other.

Moses was given the greatest and the most difficult work in his time. He was to go and deliver the children of Israel from bondage, who by law were slaves, and by culture Egyptians under the most powerful nation or government in the world. He was also to lead them to serve a living God and His government with completely different law and different culture. Moses' assignment would require a governmental power and authority greater than Egypt. Physically, there was no such government, and there was no such power and authority on the earth. Only the Kingdom of Heaven possessed such governmental power and authority to do the job. Jehovah is/was the King of Heaven and the Kingdom of Heaven. When He said, 'My presence shall be with you,' He was referring not to His omnipresence, but to His manifest presence. He was also implying that all the resources of His government, including the army in Heaven, will be available to Moses.

As we get closer and closer to the end of this age, things are going to be very, very difficult here on the earth. We need to remove our religious hypocrisy and the lame doctrinal beliefs and theological bias and reach out for the manifest presence of Jehovah and drop the counterfeit presence we have come so much to take pleasure in. Many believers say, 'Oh the presence of God was/is here.' Which type of presence are they referring to? And to what level of His presence are they referring to?

When the manifest presence of God is truly present, nothing would be impossible and there would be no power or government on earth that can match it in knowledge, wisdom, power, and authority. Things would happen not according to our earthly laws but according to heavenly laws. The resources of heaven will be deployed on earth and the works of the devil will have to take the back seat and be destroyed. Jesus Christ said, 'But if I cast out demons by the Spirit of God, surely the kingdom of God has come upon you.' (Matthew 12.28). 'For the kingdom of God is not in word but in power.' (1 Corinthians 4.20). Without the manifest presence of God, Moses' assignment would have been impossible to complete.

If the manifest presence of Jehovah was enough to set the children of Israel free under those conditions, then it will be enough to protect us and set us free from the end time afflictions and persecutions, the gloom, the darkness, and the horror of the full-blown antichrist system.

Some of the believers will be appointed and equipped to deal with the situations and circumstances of the end time. Perhaps you are a candidate. We need to prepare our hearts and minds and allow the Holy Spirit to train and transform us for the work ahead of us. We need the manifest presence of God as never before.

CHAPTER 3

The Vessel Is Made Ready

In the last chapter we saw how God revealed Himself to Moses in the burning bush and commissioned him as His prophet and ambassador to go to Egypt and deliver the children of Israel from the hard and bitter bondage and bring them before Him at Mount Sinai. Moses would have to convince Pharaoh, the king of Egypt and the most powerful king in the world at that time, to let the children of Israel go. Pharaoh was a shrewd king. He was not alone. He was supported by a powerful and well-equipped army and many demonic gods. Pharaoh was so powerful that he was feared as a god, the son of the sun god, Ra. It was in the Egyptian constitution/law to keep the children of Israel as slaves and use them to build their nation/empire. The presence of the children of Israel as slaves in Egypt also attested to the might and the glory of the king of Egypt. Pharaoh was not going to let them go without a fight.

Moses was a prince of Egypt before he became a shepherd. He knew the strength and the might of Pharaoh and of Egypt. But he was an ordinary shepherd when God commissioned him. His power and authority as a shepherd were obviously grossly negligible for his assignment. The assignment required a more powerful government than the government of Egypt, and there was none on the earth. God seemed to need a more physically powerful army and an army general to do the work; so Moses put forward serious objections to his calling. These objections are very important to everyone whom God would call and use.

In the first objection, Moses felt he was unqualified. 'Who am I that I should go to Pharaoh and that I should bring the children of Israel out of Egypt?' In other words, Moses' power and authority would be tied to who he was. Both his words and his actions would flow from who he was. Who you are is of utmost importance both in the earthly and the spiritual realms. When the sons of Sceva tried to exorcise someone in the name of Jesus, the evil spirits said, 'Jesus I know, and Paul I know; but who are you?' (Acts 19.15). In other words, the sons of Sceva did not have the power and the authorisation to cast them out. How do you see yourself? Is it in line with the way God sees you? Who are you in the spiritual realm? Answers to these questions are crucial.

The first objection also speaks of identity. God told Moses His presence was going to be with him: 'I will certainly be with you.' So identity is influenced by your fellowship and who you commune with. Moses' identity would depend on his relationship and communion with God, but not on his Hebrew origin and not on his shepherd's rod, so God was going to be his identity. God's presence with Moses was going to change his earthly source to a heavenly source of power and authority. But how was that going to help Moses practically in his new assignment?

The second question of or objection of Moses was that the children of Israel did not know God's name. 'Who is God?' The level of Moses' power and authority would be determined by the power and authority of the person who was sending him. So what was going to be Moses' supply source? This is the second most important question. What/who is your supply source?

God told him, 'I AM WHO I AM … Thus you shall say to the children of Israel, I AM has sent me to you.' (Exodus 3.14). He further told Moses, 'This is My name forever and this is My memorial to all generations.' God told Moses that His personal name was 'I AM'. We have seen from the previous chapter that the name 'I AM' means 'to exist' or 'to become'. 'I AM' is a self-existing and self-sufficient God who does not need man, animal or anything in order to exist. He is the source, beginning, and end of everything. Everything exists because of who I AM is. Nothing can exist outside of Him. He is timeless and the source of everything.

Moses was still not satisfied. He put forward a third objection to his calling. He said to God, 'But suppose they will not believe me or listen to my voice, suppose they say, 'The Lord had not appeared to you'?' (Exodus 4.1). Moses was worried about the response of the children of Israel; whether they would accept him or reject him, whether they would listen to him and obey him or brand him an impostor or a false prophet. Who are the children of Israel? Who are you sending me to? What were their beliefs, their wishes, and their expectations?

The third question or objection deals with destination or destiny. Moses was afraid of negative response and worried about his own destiny. What will happen to me? Jehovah had commissioned him as a prophet, but what had he to show for it? There must be an anchor to clinch the fact that God had sent him. Moses needed new giftings to be able to fulfil his assignment. It would be wrong for God to send someone empty-handed. God never sends anybody empty-handed, He always tailors ones gifting according his/her assignment. So if one truly finds his/her assignment or true purpose, the necessary giftings will also be present with it.

These three questions are very important to any minister of the gospel, be it a Pastor, Bishop, apostle, prophet, or any vessel whom God would use. Who are you in the spiritual realm? What is your source? What is the will of God for you, what is your fate or destiny? The answers to these questions are directly connected to one's personal interrelationship, communion, and walk with God. How much of God has rubbed off on you? How much of God do I release here on earth? You can only release here on earth what has rubbed off on you out of your relationship and fellowship with God in heaven. There must be a true relationship and a true encounter.

The second question Moses asked God was, 'Who are you?' Every minister of God must know God personally for himself/herself, not just on the pages of the Bible. The Bible was written through the inspiration of God. The Bible speaks about God, but the Bible is not God. There is a true personal living and eternal God, and we must encounter Him as a person in our own closet. It is in such a secret place that God imparts his presence, power and anointing for ministry.

There are many of us ministers who have learned the Bible and can preach reasonably well out of it, but we do not realise that God is a person and Jesus is a person apart from the Bible. The Bible gives us portals and gates through which we can enter and have communion with God and with Jesus. Do we see these portals? Have we entered these gates? We Pastors depend more on theology than experiential knowledge of God.

Many of us do not really know God as a person and Jesus as a person. God is not a written document. The letter without the Spirit is dead. God is a Person, Jesus is a Person, the Holy Spirit is a Person, and we must know them as such. The search for them must begin in our hearts. Quoting pages of the Bible alone is insufficient and using your gifts alone without communion with Jesus is also inadequate. Jesus answered such workers, 'I never knew you.' This is one of the reasons why the church is in a mess. Religion does not teach us to search for God but to be a good church goer. We teach 'churchianity' without the experience of God.

Jesus asked his disciples, 'Who do you say that I am?' It was Peter alone who responded, 'You are Christ, the Son of the living God.' Jesus said, 'Blessed are you Simon Barjonah, for flesh and blood has not revealed this to you but My Father who is in heaven. And I also say to you that you are Peter, and on this rock I will build My church and the gates of Hades shall not prevail against it.' (Matthew 16.13-18). The name Simon Barjonah symbolized his natural, humble, fleshy parental origin or DNA. However, Peter received a revelation from heaven about who Jesus really was. He would no longer be Simon Barjonah but Peter, the rock, whose source is in heaven. Upon the heavenly revelation of Jesus, who is the Rock, the church would be built, and the gates of Hades shall not prevail against it. 'And I will give you the keys of the kingdom of heaven, and whatever you bind on the earth will be bound in heaven and whatever you will loose on earth will be loosed in heaven.' (Matthew 16.19).

The Greek word translated as church is ekklesia. It means 'calling out' or 'called out'. It is a people or community called out by God out of the world, and might have been used to differentiate the church from the Jewish community. The original use of ekklesia in Athens was for a public assembly of all free citizens who had civil rights. It was not religious, but a neutral assembly, which deliberated on all matters pertaining to the state; judicial, legislative, military, welfare-related, etc. When Rome conquered Greece, it modified the concept of ekklesia to become the governing authority or state council such as the senate. The New Testament writer knew that. So, ekklesia has as its background the idea of having a governing and legislative authority and rulership.

The gate of Hades is the devil's entry point or trading floor, where demonic businesses, contracts, and agreements are conducted. If your trading floor is the heavenly kingdom, the gate of Hades shall not prevail against you. When the revelation, not the mental knowledge, of who Jesus really is dawns; then one acquires the power and authority to confront and overcome the powers of the devil. Darkness cannot prevail against light. And light will always dispel darkness.

We need not only to answer this question biblically, but also to have a revelation of who Jesus really is. Are we building our churches on the revelation of Jesus Christ or on theologies? Do our churches possess any governing authorities over forces of evil or powers of darkness? Many of our churches do not. It might be one of the reasons why the devil seems to be controlling our churches today; there is no revelation of Jesus Christ in our churches. We are not really *ekklesia* but just religious groups/clubs. There is no manifest Presence of God in our churches today. Jesus Christ worked with His apostles, confirming the word through the accompanying signs. We hardly see signs in our church services today.

We pray a lot to overcome the devil, but the greatest battle is not with the devil but with the self. The un-crucified self is blocking our spiritual advancement. We must first go to the secret place where truly God is, the most holy place. In His Sermon on the Mount, Jesus said, 'Therefore, whoever hears these sayings of Mine, and does them, I will liken him to a wise man who builds his house on the rock, and the rain descended, the flood came, and the winds blew and beat upon the house; and it did not fall, for it was founded on the rock.' (Matthew 7.24-25). We have already learnt that the rock is the revelation of Jesus. If we build on this rock, the gates of hell cannot prevail against the *ekklesia*.

The next question is, 'Who am I being sent to? What is my target? Who and what are the recipients of my calling?' Different recipients have different needs so one's purpose is tied and tailored to the recipient. If you are an apostle or a prophet, God has sent you to a particular target; it could be a local church, a community, a city, or a nation. And God would normally charge you to a particular task. Do not overstep your area of jurisdiction. It can be very dangerous when you do that. Just because you function well in your local setting does not mean you will function well in a national or global setting. My church and many other churches have paid costly prices for such unwise decisions and the activities of these misguided and overzealous ministers.

How did God continue to prepare Moses as the vessel? Every vessel God is going to use He prepares. There is no exception. God does not suddenly make someone a matured apostle, prophet, pastor etc. He trains him/her and continues to train him/her for higher offices even in the ministry. There are many people who, the moment they hear a prophecy about them, jump straight away into it. No! There is always a time of waiting; a time of preparation, a time of training. It happened to Abraham, Moses, Joseph, David, John the Baptist, Jesus Christ, Peter, Paul etc. and it will happen to you.

There are many young ministers today, perhaps because of the age in which we live, who do not take kindly to delays and waiting and training. They are in a hurry. No! It does not work that way with God; not with spiritual things. You see, God must have an image, a shadow, a likeness through which He can reveal Himself and work. Building a likeness and shadow of God in your life does not occur overnight. 'Those who wait on the Lord shall renew their strength …'

'So the Lord said to him, 'What is that in your hand?' He said, 'A rod.' And He said, 'Cast it on the ground.' So he cast it on the ground, and it became a serpent; and Moses fled from it. Then the Lord said to Moses, 'Reach out your hand and take it by the tail.' (and he reached out his hand and caught it, and it became a rod in his hand).'
Exodus 4.2-4

In Moses' hand was an ordinary dead and dry shepherd's rod with which he cared for, guided, and protected his flock. Moses had used it for many years and had not seen any special properties or powers associated with it. Without any spell, charm or incantation this dead and dry rod turned into a live snake instantly in obedience to the word of Jehovah. The DNA of the dead and dry wood was instantly transformed. The snake looked so venomous and dangerous that Moses ran from it.

God told Moses to reach out his hand and take the live snake by the tail. Moses knew that to take a live venomous snake by the tail was courting a dangerous trouble. The snake must be taken by the neck so that the head would not swing back and strike. Moses might have thought that He whose word changed a dead and dry wood into a live snake could also give him power over it. By faith Moses took the live snake by the tail and the snake turned into a rod in his hand again. Moses was beginning to walk by faith and in obedience.

The sign was primarily for the children of Israel.

Exodus 4.5

Why would the children of Israel believe the sign? What message would the sign deliver to them and point to? Why would it prove beyond doubt that Moses was a true prophet of Jehovah? The snake was the official emblem of Egypt, signifying its kingdom, power, and authority. The Israelites had seen Pharaohs wear the snake emblem on their crowns to symbolize the dominion, the power, and the authority of Egypt.

If Jehovah could take a dead and dry staff, like Pharaoh, and turn it into a powerful, wicked, evil, and fearful serpent, then He could also take the powerful, wicked, evil and fearful serpent by the tail and turn it into a dead and dry staff. It would convince the children of Israel that Jehovah was more powerful than Pharaoh and that Moses was a true prophet of Jehovah. Therefore, in the name of Jehovah, there was no need any longer to be afraid of Pharaoh and the might of Egypt. The private training of Moses had begun. Many times, God will train you in private and in silence without exposure. Do not rush to advertise yourself and your gifts until God gives the command. Many of us are doing just that; advertising our gifts before God gives a go ahead.

Moses' shepherd rod became the symbol of his new identity and also a symbol of God's power and authority. After it turned into a live snake Moses became aware that there was life hidden in the word of God and that His word can be trusted. Moses was no longer the same person. He became aware of his own ability to demonstrate the power of God. His faith in God and his own confidence might have increased tremendously. Jehovah advised him to take the rod with him to Egypt, with which he might do the signs (Exodus 4.17).

The rod was used by Moses in the miracles relating to the deliverance of the children of Israel from Egypt. It was used after their freedom from Egypt, on their way from Mount Sinai to the promised land; at the Red Sea to make a way for the children of Israel to cross, at Rephidim to bring water out of a rock for the children of Israel to drink, and to defeat the Amalekites (Exodus 14.13-15, 17.4-7, 17.8-13).

God also gave Moses a second sign.

> *'Furthermore the Lord said to him, 'Now put your hand in your bosom.' And he put his hand in his bosom, and when he took it out, behold, his hand was leprous, like snow. And He said, 'Put your hand in your bosom again.' So he put his hand in his bosom again, and drew it out of his bosom, and behold, it was restored like his other flesh. 'Then it will be, if they do not believe you, nor heed the message of the first sign, that they may believe the message of the latter sign."*
>
> Exodus 4.6-8

Leprosy was one of the worst and most dreaded diseases in Moses' time. People with leprosy were isolated, lost all contact with the community and left to die. There was no physician nor medicine or cure that could help the leprous, so they were as good as dead. Only God could heal a leper. When Moses put his hand in his cloak and brought it out, he was white with a full-blown leprosy. He was a living dead. When he put his hand back into his cloak and brought it out again, his leprosy was completely healed.

The instantaneous occurrence and healing of leprosy would be a powerful supernatural sign to Moses, and to the children of Israel, that Jehovah had power over and controlled health and disease, life and death. It would confirm Moses as a true prophet of Jehovah and also bring fear and warning to many hearts. Leprosy is a type of sin, so the sign also indicates that only God has the power to forgive and cleanse sin.

God did not stop at the second sign, He gave Moses a third sign:

> 'And it shall be, if they do not believe even these two signs, or listen to your voice, that you shall take water from the river and pour it on the dry land. The water which you take from the river will become blood on the dry land.'
>
> Exodus 4.9

Each of the signs carried a message as we have seen. The first sign carried the message of the power and authority of Jehovah over the power, authority, and the government of Egypt. The second sign carried the message of Jehovah's awesome power over health and disease, life and death. What message would the third sign carry?

The river in question was the Nile. It provided water for everyday use and for agriculture. The Nile was the source of life for the Egyptians. It was so important that the Egyptians regarded the Nile as a god. By turning the water of the Nile instantly into blood, Jehovah demonstrated that the Nile was not the source of life, but He was the source and the author of life, the 'I AM'. As Leviticus 17.11 says, 'the life of the flesh is in his blood.' It would have also demonstrated powerfully that Jehovah had power over the gods of Egypt.

A sign always directs and points to something. All the signs God gave to Moses to display in Egypt would point to Jehovah Himself, the I AM. They were meant to turn the hearts of the people, both the children of Israel and the Egyptians, to Jehovah. God gave Moses three signs, not one; He left no room for unnecessary doubt. He wanted the children of Israel and even the Egyptians to believe His word and to know Him. 'At the mouth of three the matter was confirmed, completed and sealed.' God knew the unbelief and the hardness of human hearts, especially of the children of Israel. The signs revealed some of the attributes of Jehovah and would help to bring faith to the hearts of the children of Israel.

Moses was a prince of Egypt who, 40 years ago, tried to free the children of Israel and failed. As a result, he fled and lived in Midian for those 40 years. The same Moses despite a possible danger to his life obeyed Jehovah; went back to Egypt as His prophet to free the children of Israel. Therefore, the signs gave credibility to Moses as a servant of Jehovah.

The descendants of Abraham had been strangers for four hundred years. The generation at the time of Moses had seen only servitude, slavery, hard labour, bondage, poverty, and untimely deaths. Egypt, their master, was the most powerful nation on the earth. The children of Israel might have resigned themselves to their fate and become used to their condition. Perhaps they thought their condition was their destiny and they were born to be slaves. They had to be convinced that there was another way out. Not man's way, but God's way. The children of Israel themselves had to be prepared to renew their minds and change their conditions. They had to take the supernatural lifeline God was offering to them. There was no other lifeline except the supernatural lifeline.

God knows how much and how far we have been programmed, brainwashed by our upbringing, by earthly education, culture and by the world. The word of God we hear passes through filters. We have heard it several times. We think we have got it; we think we know what God is saying, but many of us do not because of the filters. People believe they can just read the word of God or hear the word of God and get everything at once without any revelation or meditation. Some think that miracles, signs, and wonders are not for today; only the word of God is enough.

God bless them. For many people, like me, it is necessary for God to release a supernatural occurrence to make His word click, to bring understanding and a living faith which produces results. It is necessary to actually experience heaven's resources on earth. God is a Spirit but the world we live in is not, so there must be a meeting point between the spirit and the physical.

The governments of the world perhaps do their human best, but the simple fact is that none of them can truly help humanity, whether democracy, socialism, or communism. The governments, without God, are all human attempts to bring order, justice, love, and peace. None of them is perfect. None can satisfy all our needs. Like Egypt, they want to take from us to build a strong, viable and an economically thriving government. We have become pawns on the chessboard of a small elite and privileged group. We are living in Egypt and have become slaves to the Pharaohs of our day: the real powers and gods behind these world governments. Only the supernatural God can save you and me.

Those signs should have been enough for Moses, but he put forward two more objections. 'O my Lord, I am not eloquent, neither before nor since. You have spoken to Your servant; but I am slow of speech and slow of tongue.' (Exodus 4.10). Steven told the council that Moses was learned in all the wisdom of the Egyptians and was mighty in words and deeds (Acts 7.22). Did Moses suddenly lose the power of his tongue? It is uncertain.

Anyway, God assured Moses that He would be with his mouth and teach him what he should say. Then Moses said, 'O my Lord, please send by the hand of whomever else You may send.' (Exodus 4.13). Moses just did not really want to be bothered. It was too much of a risk. He did not want to leave his comfort zone. It was purely a human and common problem with most of us.

God did not absolve him of his calling. Just as God ordained and sanctified the prophet Jeremiah a prophet to the nations before he was born, so was Moses ordained and sanctified a prophet to Israel before he was born. God was patient with Moses, but He would not change his calling. It was the reason why he came to the earth anyway. God finally sent him away by appointing Aaron, his brother, as his spokesman.

We can see from the above that God needed a man to carry His manifest presence, His power, and His glory on the earth. He chose Moses to carry His manifest presence and His power on earth. Moses was born of Jewish slaves and trained in the palace of Pharaoh. Moses tried to redeem the children of Israel and failed. The time had not come for him to do that. He carried no Presence of God and no power of God. For forty years God prepared the heart of this runaway prince to carry His manifest presence and His power.

Moses wrote the first five books of the Bible. He did not have the Old Testament or the New Testament. How did Moses know about what he wrote in these books, when he was not even born? Because God showed him; because he saw them again in eternity. Eternity is timeless and has the record of everything; the past, the present and the future are all active.

Moses learnt to operate from heaven to earth and not from the earth to heaven. That was the secret of the success of Moses, the prophets, and the early apostles of the church. The early church operated from the God within to the world outside. After the church became the official religion under Constantine in 313 AD, the church began to operate in the Roman and Greek mentality. They operated from the known to the unknown; from the seen to the unseen. This is the Western way of thinking, unlike what should be: from inside, or the heavens, to the outside, or the world.

It should also be noted that the power and authority which God gave Moses was in direct relationship to his calling; in accordance with the work he was called to do. God did not give Moses a blank cheque book to do whatever he wanted with His power. God does not call you and search for what you are going to do. He calls you for a purpose and your purpose determines your anointing. If you do not know your calling, then you don't know the power and authority you possess.

One's calling begins with knowing God, and grows with walking with Him. You will not walk in the fullness or the maturity of your calling if you quit knowing God and if you fail to walk with Him. It is not just working for God but walking with Him as well. Many times, we keep too busy working for God that we miss walking with Him.

What is this treasure that is carried in earthen vessel? It is the glory of God manifested in Christ Jesus. The earthen vessel is man, man of dust. We have to learn to continually commune with, continually depend on God. We are breakable vessels. If we are not broken or humbled each time we come into God's manifest presence, then we do not really need Him anymore. If we do not need Him anymore, then we are on our own. He is no longer our source. The moment we think we have arrived and see ourselves having the ability to do what God has called us to do, we have missed God.

Take note my friend, what God has called you to do is supernatural and can only be achieved supernaturally. Take the advice from the wisdom of Solomon, 'Trust the Lord with all your heart; and lean not on your own understanding; in all your ways acknowledge Him, and he shall direct your paths.' He who has called you is the same Person who will lead and help you to achieve success. He is faithful.

CHAPTER 4

Show Me Your Glory

We have already seen that God is I AM. An invisible, self-existing and self-sustaining God who reveals Himself. Patriarchs like Enoch, Noah, and Abraham literally walked with God and pleased Him. Is it possible to literally walk with God? Yes, I believe it is. Since the first Adam and the patriarchs like Enoch, Noah and Abraham walked with God literally, it gives an indication that we too can do the same.

It is very remarkable how some of the Old Testament prophets walked so closely with God, even though the Holy Spirit had not yet returned to the earth. Their lives should inspire us all, the New Testament saints, who have received the Holy Spirit and still unable to fellowship with God as we should. Perhaps, over the years, the church has decided that it is impossible to do so and therefore blocked the way ourselves. But it is possible.

Starting from the days of Nimrod (Genesis 11) to this day, mankind has tried to fill this vacuum of intimacy with God with religion and failed. We have tried to reach God by self-effort. We try to touch God through the flesh. We have made counterfeits to quench the yearning of the soul to its origin. The spirit of man left to itself knows whence it has come and where it is supposed to go. But it seems to be trapped by his own soul. The earthen vessel must first be broken so that the light of the glory of God may be seen (2 Corinthians 4.7).

Jehovah appeared to Moses in a flame of fire from the midst of the bush. On Mount Sinai the children of Israel saw the glory of God like a consuming fire (Exodus 24.17, Deuteronomy 4.24).

Apostle Paul confirmed that God is a consuming fire (Hebrews 12.29). And Apostle John also proclaimed another revelation.

'This is the message which we have heard from Him and declare to you, that God is light and in Him is no darkness at all.'

1 John 1.5

Light can be a metaphor for goodness, excellence, purity, truth, knowledge, wisdom, holiness, and happiness, and darkness a metaphor for sin, evil, gloom, ignorance, misery, adversity, death, and the devil. Light reveals hidden things, mysteries and stores records/information and darkness holds unrevealed mysteries and hidden things. If we only interpret the revelation of John, the apostle, as a mere metaphor we shall miss a powerful revelation.

James says that God is the Father of lights (James 1.17), meaning God is the life source of every light. The Psalmist says the Lord God is clothed with honour and majesty and covered Himself with light as a garment (Psalms 104.1-2), and Paul says God dwells in inapproachable light (1 Timothy 6.16). But the beloved John sees a remarkable revelation. 'This is the message we have heard,' from whom, from Jesus Christ, the only begotten Son of God, that God is light. Not only is God the source of light, surrounded by light and dwells in light but God Himself is light. His nature is Light. The meaning of the words used for light both in the Old Testament and the New Testament is to shine and to be luminous.

So, God is a consuming fire and God is also light. Every fire gives light, and every light can produce fire (Isaiah 10.17). What does Apostle John mean when he said God is light and in Him is no darkness at all? Of course, this light is not a physical light but a spiritual light, so man cannot physically detect and/or identify this Light. There is no scientific instrument, apparatus, or mechanism that will sense and determine the nature of this Light.

God said in the beginning, "Let there be light, and there was light.' And God saw that the light was good; and God divided the light from the darkness. God called the light Day, and the darkness He called Night. So the evening and the morning were the first day.' (Genesis 1.3-5). This first light was present before God created the physical light on the fourth day (Genesis 1.14.20), so this first light was therefore uncreated.

The first uncreated light stored or held the information of the eternal records for the creation of the heaven and the earth. So, the creation of the heaven and the earth came through light. Apostle John says,

John 1.1-5

This Word, whom we know refers to Jesus Christ (John 1.14) was the light through whom everything was made. The light was the life of God and gives light (life) to every man coming into the world (John 1.9). This Light is a Person. It is alive, an uncreated Light and creative Light. The earth was created by this spiritual Light and is held in place and maintained by the same Light. It is not made of photons, as we know of natural light, but of the Life and substance of God, so it is intangible to man.

Scientists have discovered that natural light is part of an electromagnetic spectrum made up of particles (photons) with wavelike properties travelling at great speed. The human eyes can pick up only a certain range of the electromagnetic spectrum (visible rays), but there are others, like radio waves, microwaves, ultraviolet rays, X-rays, and gamma rays, which are not visible to the human eyes, even though they exist. Although all electromagnetic ranges travel at the speed of light (186,000 miles/second), each range has different wavelength and different frequency. The higher the frequency, the higher the energy they produce, and the more deadly and dangerous they become to humans.

It is also scientifically acknowledged that light is an energy source and stores and transmits information. As an energy source, light can now be used by scientists for many useful purposes, like the use of x-rays, laser, satellite, communications, and common things such as cooking. Scientists now believe that light is fundamental both to the living and to the non-living alike. The nature and the properties of light seem to underlie everything. Albeit Einstein's famous equation ($E=MC^2$) proves that light can be converted to mass; where E is energy, M is mass and C is the speed of light.

Scientists are still discovering more and more about the potential of natural light. If natural light can have such great properties and potential, it is virtually impossible to imagine the power and the potential of that spiritual Light that created the natural light. The Light, which is God, is alive, is uncreated, has no beginning. It is invisible and creative.

When God said, 'Let there be light,' and light came at the beginning of creation, the light was mixed with darkness. So God divided the light from the darkness (Genesis 1.3-5). Even the first spiritual light contained some measure of darkness. But Apostle John says, 'In Him is no darkness at all.' The Greek word for darkness is '*skotia*' meaning 'dimness,' 'obscurity' or 'darkness.' Darkness is taken by scientists as simply the absence of light, as if darkness has no form or substance.

As we have mentioned, God in the beginning divided the light from the darkness. If light had a form, so did darkness. During the deliverance of the children of Israel from Egypt, at the ninth plague, God commanded Moses to stretch out his hand towards heaven, that there may be darkness which may even be felt (Exodus 10.21). God, speaking through prophet Isaiah, says, 'I form light and create darkness, I make peace and create calamity; I, the Lord, do all these things.' (Isaiah 45.7). So, darkness may not just be the absence of light, but a form of substance still unknown to man, like dark matter.

Every light contains varying measure of darkness. 'But God is Light, and in Him is no darkness at all.' This is absolute Light, pure Light or perfect Light. Paul, speaking about his Damascus Road experience, said, 'At midday, O king, along the road I saw a light from heaven, brighter than the sun, shining around me and those who journeyed with me.' (Acts 26.13). Paul fell to the ground, and when he arose from the ground, he was blind. The sun is the source of natural light and energy for the earth, so what type of light can be brighter than the sun? It is impossible for man to imagine or determine how luminous, radiant, and bright this uncreated light can be. Apostle Paul says God, 'who alone has immortality, dwelling in unapproachable light, whom no man has seen or can see.' (1 Timothy 6.16).

The major source of light for the earth is the sun and the minor source is the moon. At times, the sun becomes so hot that its rays are damaging to the eyes and to the health of mankind. People get sunstroke and sunburn, and others even die. It indicates that natural man cannot withstand much light and/or certain ranges of the electromagnetic spectrum. If the light mixed with darkness from the created sun can be so damaging and dangerous to man, then how can man stand before an uncreated or absolute pure light which has no darkness? If therefore, man is given the grace to go close to God, he may be burnt alive at a distance by God's light. God alone is holy, separate, and unmixed. He alone is Light without any darkness in Him. I believe the type and nature of the luminous and radiance that surround God also speaks of His holiness.

The Bible says that 'Adam and his wife hid themselves from the presence of the Lord God among the tree of the garden of Eden,' and 'Cain went out from the presence of the Lord and dwelt in the land of Nod on the East of Eden.' (Genesis 3.8, 4.16). The presence of Jehovah was therefore tangible to Adam and Cain. They might have seen or felt the Presence of Jehovah or seen a form that represented His Presence.

The Hebrew word for presence is *'paniym.'* According to the Hebrew Dictionary *'paniym'* means 'face' or 'countenance'. The Scripture does not describe the face of God in these verses, but Adam and Cain saw something or some form which represented the face of God.

It was confirmed by God that Moses saw a form of Jehovah:

Numbers 12.6-8

Moses did not have a vision or a dream like a normal prophet. Either he was trans-relocated whole (spirit, soul, and body) before God, or Jehovah came down Himself to speak to Moses face to face. The Hebrew word for 'form' is *'termunah.'* According to Lexical Aid to the Old Testament, it means "something shaped, a fashioned, a form, an appearance, an image, an embodiment, a manifestation, a likeness." There are ten occurrences in the Hebrew Bible; out of which five are translated as 'likeness,' four are translated as 'similitude' and one is translated as 'image' by the KJV. Moses definitely saw Jehovah in one form or the other.

It is obvious that Moses did not see the real face of God but a form, similitude, or likeness which only Moses knew as Jehovah. Jehovah and Moses came very close to each other, that they could speak face to face. The actual Hebrew word used here for 'face' (NKJV) is *'peh,'* meaning mouth. So KJV translates it, 'with him

I speak mouth to mouth.' It meant that Jehovah spoke directly to Moses, from His mouth to Moses' mouth, without any interpretation, intermediary, interruption, misunderstanding and misconception. The question, still, is in what form did Moses see Jehovah? What did Moses see?

The children of Israel committed a terrible sin by worshipping a golden calf, so Jehovah told them He was not going to go in their midst but rather He would send His angel before the children of Israel (Exodus 33.1–3). Moses took his tent outside the camp and called it the tent of meeting.

> 'And it came to pass, when Moses entered the tabernacle [tent of meeting], that the pillar of cloud descended and stood at the door of the tabernacle, and the Lord talked with Moses … So the Lord spoke to Moses face to face, as a man speaks to his friend …'
>
> Exodus 33.9-11

In this passage we have an example of how God spoke to Moses face to face: 'The pillar of cloud descended at the door of the *tent of meeting.*' The pillar of cloud represented God's presence. So, God descended and spoke to Moses, face to face as one would speak to a friend.

> 'Then the Lord came down in the cloud, and took the spirit that was upon him, and placed the same upon the seventy elders …'
>
> Numbers 11.25

> 'Then the Lord came down in the cloud and stood in the door of the tabernacle, and called Aaron and Miriam. And both went forward.'
>
> Numbers 12.5 (see also Deuteronomy 31.15)

In all the above passages we see that Jehovah came down 'in the cloud.' The Psalmist says, 'He [God] made darkness His secret place, His canopy around Him was dark waters and thick clouds of the skies.' (Psalms 18.11). Job says, 'He covers the face of His throne and spread His cloud over it.' (Job 26.9). We have seen that Jehovah is a consuming fire and a living Light without any darkness. However, He surrounds Himself with darkness and clouds when He comes into the proximity of man.

When King Solomon placed the Ark of the Covenant in the temple he had built, the cloud filled the temple, 'so that the priests could not continue ministering because of the cloud for the glory of the Lord had filled the house of the Lord.' The cloud filled the temple because His glory had filled the temple. Then Solomon explained it in the next verse, 'The Lord said He would dwell in dark cloud.' (1 Kings 8.11-12).

Solomon was implying that the glory of the Lord was inhabiting in the cloud; the consuming Fire/Light was in the cloud. Exodus 16.10 says, 'The glory of the Lord appeared in the cloud.' So we can conclude that the glory of the Lord and/or the manifest Presence of Jehovah dwelt in the cloud. The cloud therefore can be taken both as the sign of the manifest Presence of the Lord and/or the sign of the glory of the Lord. God is not the cloud. God is within the cloud. So, Moses saw the likeness of Jehovah 'in the pillar of cloud' and they spoke to each other face to face as a friend would speak to a friend. Again, the question is what did Moses see in the cloud?

A cloud is a vaporised form of water, opaque and denser than the air, so light rays cannot go through easily. Dust and smoke can also form clouds. Jehovah therefore surrounded Himself with some form of opaque and denser material in such a way that light rays could not go through. In other words, God remained invisible, yet made it possible for man to encounter Him at various levels of sensitivity. This is very important because man, in his present constitution, cannot fully see and withstand the full radiance/brilliance of His glory. Adam and Eve hid themselves from God when they heard God approaching. God did not tell Adam anything, yet Adam was convicted and hid from God. God surrounds Himself with a cloud to hide His full glory and make intangible tangible, so that man may have an encounter with Him. Otherwise, man would be fried, burnt instantly at a distance.

The Bible says, 'Through one man sin entered the world, and death through sin, and thus death spread to all men, because all sinned.' (Romans 5.12). 'All have sinned and fallen short of the glory of God.' (Romans 3.23). 'But we are all like an unclean thing. And all our righteousnesses are like filthy rags. We all fade as a leaf. And our iniquities, like the wind, have taken us away.' (Isaiah 64.6). The common word in these Scriptures is 'all'. All have sinned. There is no exception, regardless of who you are. Nobody can stand before God's righteousness. No one!

Anytime man comes before God, he/she becomes immediately convicted. The Light/glory of God or His holiness is such that it exposes the tiniest darkness in man. Because of His love for mankind, He covers Himself with a cloud, smoke, or darkness, to tone down His glory so that He can safely commune and have fellowship with man without violating His holiness and without consuming man. Secondly, He gives man a new temporal garment of righteousness so that man can stand before Him (Zechariah 3.3-5). Anytime man presents himself before God a new temporal garment is given.

It should not be difficult now to understand why God surrounds Himself with clouds and darkness. The reason is to shade, to mute and to hide His brightness, His radiance, His holiness or who He really is so that man can still have a glimpse of what is impossible to see. The invisible can become visible, the intangible can become tangible, so that we can have a relationship with God. There is no earthly receptor or gadget which can detect the presence of God. Man, however, can detect, to some extent, the presence of God, because he is a spirit being and is light himself; made in God's image and with His DNA.

'Now the glory of the Lord rested on Mount Sinai and the cloud covered it six days. And on the seventh day He called to Moses out of the midst of the cloud. The sight of the glory of the Lord was like a consuming fire on the top of the mountain in the eyes of the children of Israel. So Moses went into the midst of the cloud and went up into the mountain. And Moses was on the mountain forty days and forty nights.'
Exodus 24.16-18

On the top of Mount Sinai, the children of Israel saw the glory of the Lord like a huge, raging and devouring fire. They saw mighty flames of fire bellowing as if in a furnace. They became afraid and could not draw near. It was different from the pillar of cloud and the pillar of fire which they had become accustomed to. God called Moses up into the fire. The first time Moses met God, he was told not to draw closer, but to remove his sandals because the place he stood was holy ground. Now God was calling him into the fire. Perhaps there was nothing in Moses for the fire to consume.

The calling of God also gave Moses a favoured ability to stand in God's glorious presence. He was given a new garment to stand in God's presence. God must call you to come. Like king of Persia, God must first extend His golden sceptre to man, otherwise he is dead (Esther 5.2). Even though the death of Jesus tore the veil from top to bottom, the Holy Spirit must give you the access. Moses had to decide for himself whether he wanted to go through the fire or not; whether he wanted to die or not. In Moses' second/third encounter with God up the mountain, the skin of his face shone with the glory of God, so that the children of Israel were afraid to go near him (Exodus 34.29-31).

Every natural fire has a source which is ignited to produce the fire, light, and heat. But Jehovah is an uncreated Fire which has no source, no beginning, and no end. He is the I AM. God is a jealous God because the fire of God would destroy anything before Him which is unholy. In one flash 50,070 men of Beth Shemesh died when they looked into the Ark of the Covenant (1

Samuel 6.19). Abihu and Nadab, children of Aaron, died on the spot when they presented profane fire before the Lord (Leviticus 10.1-2). The same fire of God covered and protected Shadrach, Meshach, and Abednego when they were put in the burning fiery furnace (Daniel 3.19-25). The furnace, heated seven times its normal use, had no effect on them; the hair of their head and their garments were not affected; not even the smell of fire was on them. To say it again, this Fire is alive. God's holiness is alive; so is God's love.

In the New Testament, John the Baptist, referring to Jesus, prophesised that 'someone was coming who would baptise with the Holy Spirit and Fire. And on the day of Pentecost there appeared to the 120 disciples divided tongues as of fire and one sat upon each of them (Acts 2.3). God had put His nature upon the disciples, but they were not consumed. That experience was the test/sign that they were born again.

Whenever there is fire, there is also light. So, whenever Jehovah manifests Himself as fire, there is also light. The glory of Jehovah cannot be fully defined and described by human language. No earthly language is adequate to describe it. Many times, there are no physical words to match or to describe the colours, the glow, the radiance, the events, and the activities. We need to rely exclusively on the Holy Spirit to give us words which can partially describe the glory of God.

Can man literally walk with God? Yes, I believe that man can literally walk with and talk to God face to face as Enoch did, as Noah did, as Abraham did and as Moses did. Although God did not reveal His complete identity to them, He gave them enough tangible presence to identify Him because of the nature of their hearts. If we search for God with all our hearts (Jeremiah 29.13), and are prepared to pay the price, he will give us our hearts' desire. We need to forget the idea that no one can see God; others in the Bible did see Him in one form or the other. And throughout church history some people have seen Him. It is our turn as believers, the true temples of God, in whom Spirit of God already dwells. If God wanted to kill us when we see Him, He wouldn't live in our hearts, and nobody could be baptized with the Holy Spirit and fire and live.

Revelation of the Glory of God

We have seen that God is a consuming Fire and God is Light, so His glory is of Fire and Light. However, the manifest presence of God appears in clouds or in some form of darkness, as we have explained above. King Solomon made a distinction between the cloud and the glory of God. He said, '… the priests could not continue ministering because of the cloud; for the glory of the Lord had filled the house of the Lord.' (1 Kings 8.11). The cloud seemed to be the reason why the priests could not continue ministering in the temple. But the cloud was the sign that the manifest presence of God had appeared. Therefore, the real reason why the priests could not continue ministering was the manifest presence of God in the cloud. The cloud hid or covered the manifest presence of the Lord and/or the glory of the Lord. The cloud therefore was the sign for both the manifest presence of the Lord and the glory of the Lord.

The obvious question is, 'Is the manifest Presence of the Lord the same as the Glory of the Lord?' My answer is no, the manifest Presence of the Lord is not the same as the glory of the Lord. The Glory of the Lord always incorporates as one, all the attributes of God including the manifest Presence of the Lord. Where the Glory of the Lord is, the manifest Presence of the Lord is also there. But the manifest Presence of the Lord does not necessarily have to be the Glory of the Lord. Jehovah appeared to Moses in a burning bush on Mount Sinai, but when he stood on the same mountain with the children of Israel about six months later, the appearance of the Lord was not the same and Moses became exceedingly afraid and trembled (Hebrews 12.21). Moses saw God's manifest presence the first time and His glory the second time.

So, what is the glory of God or the glory of the Lord? The Hebrew word for glory is '*kabowd.*' It means 'weight,' 'honour,' 'glory,' 'esteem,' 'splendour,' 'majesty,' 'beauty,' 'magnificence,' 'abundance,' and 'wealth.' When Jehovah manifests His glory, He manifests His weight and heaviness, His splendour, His majesty, His magnificence, His wealth and His fullness. In His glory all His attributes are manifested at the same time. In His Presence some of His attributes are displayed, but not all of them. Therefore, the Glory of the Lord reveals something far more than His manifest Presence. In His glory, the Lord shows off Himself, His true invisible nature, His true value and His true worth, His fullness, His inner total Self. But who can stand His fullness? In His glory, the Lord shows what makes Him who He is, what makes Him the only God. To say it in a common language, what makes Him tick. The manifest presence and the glory of the Lord are different levels of revelation of the same God.

No human being or language can therefore fully define or describe the glory of God in its fullness. No one can know God in His fullness because one has to be in the same realm to know it. God is the source of all things and no man, or any created thing, can see His fullness. However, there seems to be a progressive revelation of God in the Bible. The pillar of the cloud and the pillar of fire was a symbol of the presence of God, and it led the children of Israel for 50 days from Egypt to Mount Sinai. The children of Israel could see the pillar of the cloud and the pillar of fire above them, and they might have taken it for granted, but on Mount Sinai they could not. 'The sight of the glory of the Lord was like a consuming fire on top of the mountain in the eyes of the children of Israel.' (Exodus 24.17).

The children of Israel were terrified and could not go near the glory of the Lord. Moses warned the children of Israel to take heed, for the Lord their God was a consuming Fire, a jealous

God (Deuteronomy 4.24, Hebrews 12.29-29). He possessed the ability to consume and to burn them alive.

In the vision of the glory of the Lord, prophet Isaiah saw the Lord sitting on a throne, high and lifted up and the train of His robe filled the temple. Above it stood seraphim and one of them cried and another said, 'Holy, Holy, Holy is the Lord of hosts; the whole earth is full of your glory.' (Isaiah 6.2-3). When Isaiah saw the vision, he was convicted: 'Woe is me, for I am undone! Because I am a man of unclean lips, and I dwell in the midst of a people of unclean lips; for my eyes have seen the King, the Lord of hosts.' (Isaiah 6.5). Prophet Isaiah revealed that the glory of the Lord was the glory of His kingship. The glory of the King should be reflected in the lives of His people. And Isaiah lamented of the lack of that reflection in his life and the lives of his people.

Prophet Daniel saw the Ancient of Days seated on His throne. His garment was white as snow, and His hair was like pure wool. His throne was fiery flame and its wheels a burning fire. A fiery stream issued and came forth from before Him. A thousand thousands ministered to Him; ten thousand times ten thousand stood before Him. The court was seated, and the books were open.

In the vision of Apostle John, he saw the throne of God, and He who sat on it was 'like a jasper and a Sardis stone in appearance. And the glow of an emerald surrounded the throne like a rainbow. From the throne proceeded lightnings, thunderings, and voices. Four living creatures were around the throne and seven lamps of fire were burning before the throne.' The four living creatures do not rest day and night, saying; 'Holy, holy, holy, Lord God Almighty, who was and is and is to come!' (Revelations 4.3-8). He also saw Elders around the throne and ten thousand times ten thousand praising God.

All the descriptions of the glory of God by Isaiah, Daniel and John depicted the grandeur, the power, the authority, the majesty and the splendour and the government of a King on His throne. The glory of a king includes his wealth and his domain; his people and his territory. You can see that the glory of the Lord is far greater in radiance, brilliance, wealth, majesty and splendour; far more extensive than the manifest presence of the Lord.

The consuming fire on Mount Sinai with thunders, lightings, trumpets and clouds made the children of Israel draw back in fear. The Lord on His throne and His robe filling the temple and the posts vibrating with the voice of seraphim, made prophet Isaiah shout, 'Woe is me, for I am undone!' The glory of God with seraphim attending, His likeness as jasper and Sardis stones, with lightnings flashing and thunders sounding, with twenty-four elders in white robes wearing golden crowns, falling down before Him, presented an atmosphere of majesty, awe, grandeur with explosive array of light displays. One needs the grace of God to even glimpse and withstand the glory of God.

There is always light, fire, radiance, brilliance or splendour accompanying the glory of God. When the glory of God is revealed on the earthly realm it is also accompanied by some level of cloud or darkness. In other words, the glory of God goes through some form of shading of various levels before it is revealed on the earth. God is omnipresent. He is everywhere in His fullness at the same time and there is no place He is not. In His omnipresence man does not know Him, see Him, nor sense Him. He is far beyond our tangible recognition. But when His glory manifests Himself, He comes down in clouds/darkness to our level and His presence becomes revealed and tangible. We can then perceive, see, and know, commune with, feel, and sometimes touch Him.

The manifestation of the glory of God produces an atmosphere charged with God's presence, power, and authority and all His attributes. Under the atmosphere of the glory of God, His will is instantly carried out, His authority is instantly enforced, His sovereignty is immediately displayed, and His government is totally in session.

The glory of God is sometimes described or defined as the atmosphere of heaven or the atmosphere of the kingdom of God. When it is defined in such terms, it is not referring to the weather but the atmosphere the glory of God brings or the influence the glory of the Lord produces on the earth. In this atmosphere, nothing is impossible; there is no disorder, no disease, no bondage, and no devil. In this atmosphere the kingdom of God is fully manifested, and all things are possible. This is why it is absolutely necessary in the last days to be following the glory of God.

When the children of Israel sinned by worshipping the golden calf, God told them to leave Mount Sinai and that He would send His angel to go with them to the promised land. But He would not go with them. 'Go up to a land flowing with milk and honey; for I will not go up in your midst, lest I consume you on the way, for you are a stiff-necked people.' (Exodus 33.3). Moses pleaded thus with God after the sin of the golden calf:

> 'Now therefore, I pray, if I have found grace in Your sight, show me now Your way, that I may know You and that I may find grace in Your sight. And consider that this nation is your people.'
>
> Exodus 33.13

The Hebrew word for grace is *'chen'. It means 'favour,' 'kindness,' 'grace,' 'loveliness,' 'charm,' and 'preciousness.' Moses pleased God and was accepted by God. He spoke to Moses face to face as a man would speak to his friend (Exodus 33.11). Moses therefore already had an unparalleled relationship and communion with God. So, he began from that basis: 'If I have found grace in Your sight show me Your way.'*

The Hebrew word 'way' is 'derek.' 'Derek' means 'a trodden road;' figuratively a course of life or mode of action. And the Hebrew word 'know' is 'yada,' meaning 'to ascertain by sight,' 'to perceive,' 'to discern,' and 'to be acquainted with.' Moses was asking God to show him a spiritual trodden path or mode of action that would lead him to have a greater personal and intimate knowledge of Him. The greater personal and intimate knowledge of God would also bring greater grace which might change the stand God had taken in connection with the sin of the children of Israel. In other words, Moses was interceding and trying to find more grace, not only for himself but for the rest of the children of Israel. Moses was showing his priestly and intercessory character.

God's reply was, 'My Presence will go with you, and I will give you rest.' (Exodus 33.14). God saw the heart of Moses and the grace of God upon his life was extended to the rest of the children of Israel. Moses continued his mediation.

> 'If Your Presence does not go with us, do not bring us up from here. For how then will it be known that Your people and I have found grace in your sight, except You go with us? So we shall be separate, Your people and I, from all the people who are upon the face of the earth.'
>
> Exodus 33.15-16

Moses was revealing that it was the manifest Presence of God which would bring the grace. It would consecrate them, protect them, provide for them and give the children of Israel a new and unparalleled level of identity. Remember the manifest presence can also be identified with the glory of God. Without the manifest Presence of God, the children of Israel were just like any other people, any other nation, depending on their own strength and wisdom. The manifest Presence would bring in the resources of the kingdom of God for their favour. If a church does not normally have the manifest Presence of God in its services, then the 'church' does not belong to God. It is not a church. Perhaps it is some kind of a social club or an organisation calling itself a 'church'. It is on its own.

The Lord said to Moses, 'I will also do this thing you have spoken; for you have found grace in My sight, and I know you by name.' (Exodus 33.17). God had restored His very presence in the midst of Israel on account of Moses. The grace of God upon one man changed the course of history for the children of Israel.

Moses went further and made another startling request, 'Please show me Your glory.' Now, Moses was the only man who saw a form of Jehovah and spoke to Him face to face. He had seen the manifest Presence of God many times. But he desired to see more than the form, more than the shadow and the similitude. He asked to see Jehovah without the form and without the cloud. He wanted to see His real face.

God's answer was, "I will make all My goodness pass before you and I will proclaim the name of the Lord before you. I will be gracious to whom I will be gracious and I will have compassion on whom I will have compassion.' But He said, 'You cannot see My face, for no man can see my face and live." (Exodus 33.19-20).

The Hebrew word used for 'face' is the same *paniym,* we have seen before, translated as Presence. This confirms the fact that the manifest Presence of God Moses had been seeing in the cloud was not the glory of God or His real face but an image, a shadow or a similitude. God had already said His Presence would go with Moses and the children of Israel, so Moses was asking for something greater than His Presence.

Jehovah did not completely refuse Moses. He said, 'I will make all My goodness pass before you and I will proclaim the name of the Lord before you. I will be gracious to whom I will be gracious and I will have compassion on whom I will have compassion.'

'No man can see my face and live.' The Hebrew word for man is Adam. In other words, no man with Adamic nature can see My real face and live. Does it imply that believers, who are dead to self, who have shed and don't operate in the Adamic nature, can see His face? This is a very difficult question to answer. We press in, and ask, and seek and knock. If we are serious and very diligent, God will reveal 'Himself,' but at the end of the day, there is something about God man will never know. Man can be like God, but man will never be God. So let us stop playing God and let God be God.

Apostle Paul speaking of God says, 'who alone has immortality, dwelling in unapproachable light, whom no man has seen or can see.' (1 Timothy 6.16). The Greek word for man here is *anthropos*. *Anthropos* means a human being, man in distinction from gods, animals and other living being. So *anthropos* is an ordinary man. In such a form he/she cannot see God. After the dead of Jesus, the veil in the temple was torn from top to bottom, and believers became the temple of the living God. The glory of God is within every believer but unmanifested. The level of the real-time revelation we have of God varies from person to person and is determined by various factors such as intimacy, relationship, obedience, and death to self and others, but His presence is accessible to every believer.

The name of a person gives an indication of who he is, his power and his authority. Nobody knew God's real name except what He told Moses, 'I AM'. Jehovah was going to proclaim His name as He passed by for Moses to know who He was. That revelation would embody all His goodness. It meant the central core of His being, His true essence, expressing all His goodness. This intrinsic goodness is encapsulated by the pronouncement, 'I will be gracious to whom I will be gracious and I will have compassion on whom I will have compassion.' I describe this as the Sovereign Love of God. All the goodness of God is borne out of love. All the goodness of God is love.

As God promises Moses, He descended in the cloud and stood with Moses. He passed by Moses and proclaimed His name.

This is the full name of God; the sevenfold name of God. He
cut it short as 'I AM' for Moses and the children of Israel, but
now He pronounced it in full. The first part of the name; 'merciful and gracious, longsuffering, and abounding in goodness and
truth, keeping mercy for thousand, forgiving iniquity and transgression and sin' can be categorised as the sovereign love of God.
And the second part; 'by no means clearing the guilty, visiting
the iniquity of the fathers upon the children and the children's
children to the third and the fourth generation' can be categorised as an aspect of His holiness.

So, the intrinsic nature of God or His real essence can be described as Love and Holiness. God is love (1 John 4.8, 16). God
is holy (Psalms 99.9, 1 Peter 1.15-16). The essence of the glory
of the Lord is Love and Holiness. The purpose of His glory is to
show His Love and His Holiness in its fullness. Everything God
did and will do flows out of love and holiness. The manifestation
of God as a consuming Fire and as Light is an expression of His
Love and Holiness.

'He who does not love does not know God, for God is love.' (1
John 4.8). 'And we have known and believed the love that God
has for us. God is love, and he who abides in love abides in God
and God in him.' (1 John 4.16). The Psalmist says, 'Exalt the Lord
our God, and worship at His holy hill; for the Lord our God is
holy.' (Psalms 99.9). Joshua warned the children of Israel, 'You
cannot serve the Lord, for He is a holy God. He is a jealous God.
He will not forgive your transgressions nor your sins.' (Joshua
24.19). Hannah praised the Lord and said, 'No one is holy like

the Lord. For there is none besides You, nor is there any rock like our God.' (1 Samuel 2.2).

God cannot do anything except out of His dual nature of love and holiness. Sometimes unbelievers, and some believers, ask, 'Well, if God is love, why are bad things happening?' They forget that God is also holy and many times, we ourselves have given the devil permission to legally afflict us. Unknown to many of us, many of the bad things happening in the world today are the cumulative consequences of thousands of years of sin or lawlessness; so are righteousness, goodness, and love. Sin and bad things, righteousness, goodness, and love do not only affect individuals or few people, they add to the general atmosphere in families, communities, cities, and nations, and their consequences affect innocent people and are passed from generation to generation.

It is the nature of God to judge, chastise, punish, destroy, and even send people to hell as part of His love and holiness. But it is also His nature to save, protect, bless, favour, empower, and defend people. Every one of us has a free will, which God will not violate, but we are responsible for our thoughts, our words, and our deeds individually and collectively.

Moses saw the goodness of Jehovah pass before him as he heard the proclamation of God's name. God is pure eternal Light, and light reveals hidden mysteries and stores information/records. So, Moses saw the full records of the future in real-time. He saw the coming of Jesus, His death, and the salvation of mankind. Jehovah also said, 'So it shall be, while My glory passes by that I will put you in the cleft of the rock and will cover you with My hand while I pass by. Then I will take away My hand and you shall see My back, but My face shall not be seen.' (Exodus 33.22-23).

Peter, at the Pentecost, said Jesus was the prophetic fulfilment of the stone which was rejected by the builders that became the chief cornerstone. The cleft symbolises Jesus' broken body, His death. It points to the fact that only through the death and the blood of Jesus Christ can one have a true glimpse of the glory of God. So, it was pointing to our time. Moses saw the time of Jesus and our time.

As Moses saw the back parts of Jehovah God, he saw also all the past records of His goodness in real-time. That was why Moses was able to write the creation of the heaven and earth in Genesis as if he were present and write about his death in the book of Deuteronomy while still alive. God also declares the end from the beginning (Isaiah 46.10). Moses, in that brief moment, saw the past, the present and the future of the goodness of Jehovah in real-time. Moses saw the extent of God's love and holiness, and he bowed his head towards the earth and worshipped God. Worship is therefore the first and the proper response to the glory of God.

On the high mountain Jesus was transfigured before His disciples. His face shone like the sun and His clothes became as white as light. Apostle Paul says, 'Christ in you, the hope of glory.' The glory of God in Jesus was manifested to His disciples. Jesus on the mountain gave us an example of the true matured sons of God. Yes, we can also be transformed into the likeness of Jesus. 'As He is, so are we in this world.'

As we get closer to the end of time God is going to do a new thing. The glory of God will first flow from within us and touch the world. God is going to use His matured sons to release the glory and bring in the end time revival and the end time harvest. 'Out of your heart will flow rivers of living water.' You are praying for revival? This last revival will flow through you and me. Believe it and prepare for it. It is coming. 'For behold, the darkness shall cover the earth, and deep darkness the people; but the Lord will arise over you and His glory will be seen upon you. The Gentiles shall come to your light and the kings to the brightness of your rising.' (Isaiah 60.2-3).

The Abiding Glory

God told Moses, 'And this shall be a sign to you that I have sent you: When you have brought the people out of Egypt, you shall serve me on this mountain.' (Exodus 3.12). When the children of Israel reached the mountain, the first thing God did was to send them a proposal: 'Now therefore if you will indeed obey My voice and keep My covenant, then you shall be a special treasure to Me above all people; for all the earth is Mine. And you shall be to Me a kingdom of priests and a holy nation.' (Exodus 19.5-6). Israel was to serve God as a kingdom of priests and a holy nation.

A kingdom is a king and his dominion. It is a king influencing his domain and his subjects with his nature, character, and desires in a governmental protocol. The King, who in this case was God, wanted His subjects to first minister to Him as priests. The priests would have the grace to commune with God first and then become mediators and intercessors between God and man. If Israel would obey the King's voice and keep His covenants, then their King will manifest His nature, character, and desires in their lives. In that way Israel will be a holy nation, as God is holy, and be able to extend God's nature, character, and desires to the rest of the nations of the earth.

When Israel accepted the proposal, God came down Himself on Mount Sinai on the fiftieth day (after they left Egypt) in the eyes of all the children of Israel.

'And Moses brought the people out of the camp to meet with God, and they stood at the foot of the mountain. Now Mount Sinai was completely in smoke because the Lord descended upon it in fire. Its smoke ascended like the smoke

Exodus 19.16-20

God's manifest presence on Mount Sinai was completely different from the burning bush experience of Moses and from the pillar of cloud and the pillar of fire the children of Israel were used to. It was the most fearsome experience. When the children of Israel saw the thick cloud, thunder, lightning, the smoke, the fire, the quaking of the mountain, and the blasting of the trumpet, they became afraid and terrified. They had never seen God manifest Himself in such a way, so they stood far away in fear. 'The sight of the glory of the Lord was like a consuming fire on top of the mountain in the eyes of the children of Israel.' (Exodus 24.17).

We have seen that the intrinsic nature of God is love and holiness. On Mount Sinai the holiness of God was much more displayed in contrast to His intrinsic nature of love. As powerful and fearsome as it was, the revelation of God or the glory of God on Mount Sinai did not have any divine structure to dwell in. There was no blood protocol to allow God to intimately connect with man. Man was still sin, under the sentence of death (Romans 6.23, Romans 5.12).

However, a special bond and union between God and the children of Israel began to be formed on Mount Sinai. That special relationship could best be described as a 'marriage covenant.' The Torah and all the statutes and ordinances later became part of the 'marriage contract.' God is a holy God, a consuming Fire and a Jealous God. For Him to have that type of relationship with the children of Israel, they had to live in a covenant relationship, submissive to God in accordance to His holiness. They would then become 'a kingdom of priests and a holy nation,' distinct from all other nations.

Moses wrote down the law, the statutes, and the ordinances in a book, built an altar, and offered burnt offerings and peace offerings on it. He sprinkled the altar with blood. Then he read the book of the covenant to the children of Israel and sprinkled them with the rest of the blood, saying, 'This is the blood of the covenant which the Lord has made with you according to all these words.' (Exodus 24.4-8). The 'marriage covenant' between God and the children of Israel was ratified by blood. God was legally 'married' or bound to the children of Israel and the children of Israel bound to God under a 'marriage covenant,' of which the Torah or the Law was the central text.

The Torah was not just a set of rules but an image through which the children of Israel could walk in God's nature, commune with Him and receive the benefits of their King from heaven. It will not be wrong to say that the law was the image, the nature, the character of the King-God. What did Jesus Say? He had come not to destroy the law and the prophets but to fulfil them. 'He is the end of the law for everyone who believes.' Jesus Christ became the law, the final image of the King in heaven on the earth. We should be very careful when we begin to throw away everything about the Old Testament as irrelevant.

When the 'marriage covenant' was ratified, then and only then did Jehovah ask Moses to build Him a sanctuary, that He, the Holy One, might dwell among them. Dwelling among them was the only way the 'marriage' between Jehovah and the children of Israel could be consummated.

> *'Speak to the children of Israel that they bring me an offering ... and let them make me a sanctuary that I may dwell among them, according to all that I show you, that is, the pattern of the tabernacle and the pattern of all its furnishings, just so you shall make it.'*
>
> Exodus 25.2-9

The sanctuary, the dwelling place of God, was to be built according to the pattern in heaven. The sanctuary or the tabernacle consisted of three parts, the outer court, the inner court or the Holy Place, the Holy of Holies and the Most Holy Place. While the sanctuary can refer to the whole tabernacle, it properly referred to the most holy place where the Ark of the Covenant was kept.

The Ark of the Covenant was a wooden box overlaid with pure gold (Exodus 25.12-15), into which was placed the tablet of the law. Later on, God instructed Moses to include the pot of manna and Aaron's lively rod. The Ark of the Covenant symbolised Christ in His humanity and in His divinity. On top of the Ark of the Covenant was the mercy seat.

The mercy seat was the lid of the Ark of the Covenant, made of pure solid gold (no wood), continuous with two cherubim in one piece. 'And you shall make two cherubim of gold; of hammered work you shall make them at the ends of the mercy seat … the cherubim shall stretch out their wings, and they shall face one another, the faces of the cherubim shall be toward the mercy seat.' (Exodus 25.18-20). The mercy seat depicted the perfect divinity of Jesus. It provided a covering for the contents of the Ark of the Covenant, especially the tablet of the law. Therefore, the law, the Torah, was covered by the divinity of Jesus Christ.

The two cherubim also made of solid gold represented special angelic beings always connected to the glory of God. They faced each other and looked towards the centre of the mercy seat where the blood of atonement was applied. 'You shall put the mercy seat on top of the ark … and there I will meet with you, and I will speak with you from above the mercy seat, from between the two cherubim which are on the ark of the Testimony, about everything which I will give you in commandment to the children of Israel.' (Exodus 25.21-23). The glory of God appeared between the two cherubim on top of the mercy seat and spoke to Aaron, the high priest. The children of Israel referred to Jehovah as the Lord who dwells between the cherubim (1 Samuel 4.4, Psalms 80.1, Psalms 99.1).

In Hebrew, the word for 'dwell' in the above verses is '*yashab*.' It implies sitting down, enthroned, as a Judge or a King. So the mercy seat could be seen as the throne of Jehovah, where He administrated His kingdom. The Ark of the Covenant and the mercy seat together symbolised the glory of the Lord and the centre of the government of Jehovah. Jehovah asked for a dwelling place, a throne, in a movable tent because Israel was on the move and had not come to her rest. The Most Holy Place, where the glory of God usually appeared, was so holy that Aaron was allowed in the place only once a year, during the Day of Atonement. He had to prepare himself meticulously for seven days before going in, otherwise he would die.

'Tell Aaron your brother not to come at just any time into the Holy place inside the veil, before the mercy seat which is on the ark, lest he die, for I will appear in the cloud above the mercy seat.'

Leviticus 16.2

The Most Holy Place and the Holy Place were separated by a thick veil, woven of blue, purple, and scarlet thread, fine linen, and artistic designs of cherubim (Exodus 26.31). Rabbinical writings state the veil was so strong that two teams of oxen could not tear it apart. In Herod's temple it was 60 feet tall, very strong and heavy. When Jesus died on the cross 'the veil of the temple was torn in two from top to bottom ...' The veil symbolised the flesh of Jesus. 'Therefore, brethren, having boldness to enter the Holiest by the blood of Jesus by a new and living way which He consecrated for us, through the veil, that is His flesh.' (Hebrews 10.19-20).

Immediately when Aaron entered the Holy of Holies, he would put incense on the fire in his censure, 'that the cloud of incense may cover the mercy seat that is in the testimony, lest he dies.' (Leviticus 16.13). God would appear in the cloud and see Aaron through the cloud of incense. The incense put on the fire to produce the cloud represented the suffering and the death of Jesus

Christ. The high priest could only see the glory of God or the manifestation of God through the symbol of the sacrifice of Jesus. The cloud, as we have discussed, would hide the full manifestation of the Lord.

God told Moses to make the tabernacle according to the pattern He had shown him on the mountain. Outside the tabernacle the children of Israel were camped round the tabernacles in their tribes. On the east were Issachar, Judah, and Zebulun. The head was Judah, and the emblem of Judah was a lion. On the west were Benjamin, Ephraim, and Manasseh. The head was Ephraim, and the emblem of Ephraim was an ox. On the north side were Asher, Dan, and Naphtali. The head was Dan, and the emblem of Dan was an eagle. On the south were Gad, Reuben, and Simeon. The head was Reuben, and the emblem of Reuben was a man. The four major emblems around the tabernacle, the lion, the ox, the eagle, and the man, corresponded exactly to the heads of the living creatures found in the visions of Ezekiel and John. These were the four sides or faces of the representation and revelation of God.

When the children of Israel finished preparing the tabernacle, the Lord spoke to Moses,

> 'On the first day of the first month you shall set up the tabernacle of the tent of meeting. You shall put in it the ark of the Testimony, and partition off the ark with the veil.'
>
> Exodus 40.2

Moses set up all the furnishing of the tabernacle in the outer court, the inner court and the Most Holy Place and consecrated and hallowed everything with anointing oil. Secondly, Aaron and his sons were brought, washed with water, clothed with their priestly garments, and anointed with oil to consecrate them to minister to the Lord as priests. Aaron was to be the High Priest, his sons the priests, and the rests of the Levi family to serve various duties in the tabernacle. The Levites were chosen to work in the tabernacle instead of the firstborn sons of Israel because they distinguished themselves from the incidence of the worship of the golden calf at Mount Sinai.

The holiness of God required the shedding of blood for Him to dwell among men. It necessitated the Levitical order of priesthood to handle the blood and sacrifices and to mediate between God and man. Moses offered burnt offering and the grain offering as instructed by God.

> 'Then the cloud covered the tabernacle (ohel) of meeting and the glory of the Lord filled the tabernacle (mishkan). And Moses was not able to enter the tabernacle of meeting because the cloud rested above it, and the glory of the Lord filled the tabernacle.'
>
> Exodus 40.34-35

A year earlier the Lord had changed the calendar of the Jews. 'This month shall be to you your beginning of months; it shall be the first month of the year to you.' (Exodus 12.2). Exactly a year later it should have been an anniversary celebration of their freedom, the change of the calendar and their new hope; a remembrance of the fearful and consuming God on the top of the mountain and the giving of the law. But instead, it was a beginning of another new institution; God with us, Emmanuel. God began to dwell among His people. It was a resetting of their calendar, hopes and their horizons. Their new calendar began with Jehovah God dwelling in their midst.

There was now a structure for Jehovah God to dwell in and there was the atoning blood between Jehovah God and the children of Israel and the mediation role of the Levitical priesthood. Jehovah could dwell in their midst because of the blood. One finds that the manifestation of God's holiness as we saw on Mount Sinai, in the form of the consuming fire, had been toned down through the blood of the sacrificial system. God was beginning

104

to manifest His love through the sacrifices and not only His holiness. Jehovah God and man were much closer in the tabernacle than they were on Mount Sinai. But make no mistake about it, the fire of God's holiness was as potent as ever. Aaron was to find out the hard way when his two sons, Nabab and Abihu, were killed by God's holiness when they took unauthorised fire before the Lord (Leviticus 10.1-2, Numbers 26.20).

Two different Hebrew words are translated as tabernacle in the above scripture (Exodus 40.34-35). '*Ohel*' refers to the entire outside complex of the dwelling place of God and '*Mishkan*' refers to the tent inside the complex. This tent, the tent of meeting, was divided by a thick veil into the Holy Place and the Most Holy Place. The Ark of the Covenant, including the mercy seat symbolising the glory of the Lord, was located in the Most Holy Place.

At the first inauguration of the dwelling place of God, the last incense and the last sacrifice offered, Moses and the priests, having finished, left the tabernacle. Then suddenly the cloud which had previously led the children of Israel and recently settled on Moses' temporary tent of meeting outside the camp (Exodus 33.7-9) began to move and covered the tent and the whole tabernacle, while the light of God's glory, which was noticed on Mount Sinai, moved and filled the newly constructed tent. Moses tried to re-enter the tabernacle but could not because the cloud was over it and the glory of God had filled the tent (Exodus 40.34-35, See also Numbers 9.15-16). It seemed to suggest that the revelation of the glory of God in the Most Holy Place was far greater than on Mount Sinai.

The cloud of God remained over the tabernacle, but the glory of God which had filled the tent later moved into the Most Holy place to allow the priests to do their work.

*'Whenever the cloud was taken up from above the tabernacle [**mishkan**], the children of Israel would go onward in their journeys. But if the cloud was not taken up,*

Exodus 40.36-38

The children of Israel had the cloud of God in sight for the rest of their journeys. Now the tent where the glory of God dwelt became their focus, and the children of Israel began to follow the cloud above it. The cloud, however, veiled the glory of God in the Most Holy Place. So, the children of Israel followed the glory of God throughout their journeys. Amazing!

We, the believers, have become the temple of God, the glory of God is within us, and this is where we should begin to locate and follow the glory of God; from within. The cloud above the tent was no longer in sight after the children of Israel reached the Promised Land. A permanent location was chosen for the tabernacle. But the cloud and the glory of the Lord still appeared in the Most Holy Place, on top of the mercy seat in the temple.

The Jewish Rabbis coined an extra-biblical word for the abiding or the dwelling manifestation of the glory of the Lord. They called it Shekinah glory. Although the word Shekinah is not in the Bible, the concept of the abiding glory of the Lord is in the Bible; in the Most Holy Place.

Some commentators identify the Shekinah glory with the glory in the Most Holy place in the tabernacle of Moses and in the temple of Solomon. Others include the glory of the Lord at Mount Sinai. Whatever way we look at it, once the tabernacle of Moses was erected and set up; Jehovah had a dwelling place in the midst of His people. The tabernacle was the symbol of Jesus Christ.

When the First Temple was built by King Solomon, the Ark of the Covenant and all the furnishing of the Moses' tabernacle were brought and placed into the temple. It was really David who received the divine pattern of the Temple and gave it to his son Solomon; so the divine pattern of the tabernacle in heaven was maintained in the construction of the Temple, and the blood sacrifices were also maintained. The Shekinah glory came into the Temple during the dedication of Solomon's Temple, as it did when Moses' tabernacle was dedicated.

> 'When Solomon had finished praying, fire came down from heaven and consumed the burnt offering and the sacrifices, and the glory of the Lord filled the temple. And the priests could not enter the house of the Lord, because the glory of the Lord had filled the Lord's house.'
>
> 2 Chronicles 7.1-2; 1 Kings 8.10-13

The Shekinah glory came to abide in the Temple and it became the permanent dwelling place of God. The Shekinah glory of the Lord had journeyed from Mount Sinai in a fearful, terrifying manifestation, then in the tabernacle of Moses until the children of Israel reached the Promised Land. In the promise land the glory of the Lord dwelt first in the localised place in Shiloh, then in the tabernacle of David on Mount Zion, and permanently in the Temple of Solomon. However, the ultimate habitation of the glory of God is man and the body of Christ. 'Do you not know that you are the temple of God and that the Spirit of God dwells in you?'

Man, the True Temple of God

Though the glory of the Lord had a permanent rest place in the temple, it was still a shadow of what was to come.

Paul declares that God does not dwell in temples made with hands nor worshipped with men's hands (Acts 17.24). The real and the original intent of God was to dwell in man again as He did in the first Adam and restore the lost oneness with Him and the dominion of mankind. God created man according to the same pattern of the tabernacle and the temple. 'And the Lord God formed man of the dust of the ground, and breathed into his nostrils the breath of life; and man became a living soul.' Man became a tri-partite being (1 Thessalonians 5.23). He is a spirit, having a soul and living in a body.

As the glory of God dwelt in the Most Holy Place in the tabernacle and the Temple, so the glory of God dwells in the spirit of a believer, not in his soul and not in his body. 'For You Have made him a little lower than the angels, and you have crowned him with glory and honour. You have made him to have dominion over the works of Your hands; You have put all things under his feet.' (Psalms 8.5-6). The Hebrew word for 'angels' is Elohim. The same Hebrew word for God. So, God made Adam/mankind a little lower than Himself and crowned him with glory and honour. The Hebrew word for crowned is *atar*, meaning to surround; so the glory of God that was in Adam's spirit extended out over his soul and his body. It was the glory of God that first engaged the world and brought the kingdom of God to bear on the earth.

When the Adam sinned, the result was catastrophic.

1. The Spirit of God left.
2. Adam died. Cut off from God.
3. Adam lost his dominion/authority/influence and therefore lost his own kingdom.
4. The devil took Adam's kingdom and began to rule the earth. Even though the earth still belonged to God, the world was no longer under God's heavenly government but under the devil's demonic earthly government.

In the Old Testament, the Spirit of God came upon special people like the priests, kings, and prophets, but He could not live within man. But God promised that He would send again the Spirit of God to live in man. 'I will put My Spirit within you and cause you to walk in My statutes, and you will keep My judgements and do them. Then you shall dwell in the land that I gave to your fathers; you shall be My people, and I will be your God.' (Ezekiel 36.27-28). Jesus Christ reiterated the Fathers promise, 'And I will ask the Father, and He will give you another Comforter [Counsellor, Helper, Intercessor, Advocate, Strengthener and Standby] that He may remain with you forever – The Spirit of truth whom the world cannot receive [welcome, take to its heart] because it does not see Him and know and recognise Him. But you know and recognise Him for He lives with you [constantly] and will be in you.' (John 14.16-17 AMP).

Prophet Joel further prophesied that the Spirit of God will not only come upon special people but all people. 'And it shall come to pass afterwards that I will pour out my Spirit upon all flesh; your sons and daughters shall prophesy, your old men shall dream dreams, your young men shall see visions.' (Joel 2.28). Jesus Christ told his disciples to wait for the enduement of power. 'Behold, I send the Promise of My Father upon you; but tarry in the city of Jerusalem until you are endued with power from on high.' (Luke 24.49).

After Jesus Christ took the sin of mankind, paid the ultimate price on the cross, took the keys from the devil (Revelations 1.18) and resurrected, He breathed into His disciples just as The Lord God breathed into the first Adam. 'Peace to you! As the Father has sent Me, I also send you,' and when He had said this, He breathed on them, and said to them, 'receive the Holy Spirit.' (John 20.21-22). Paul asks, 'Do you not know that your body is the temple of the Holy Spirit who is in you whom you have from God and you are not your own?' (1 Corinthians 6.19).

Jesus, for 40 days after His resurrection, instructed his disciples about the kingdom of God. Ten days after His ascension into heaven (50 days after His resurrection), He poured the Holy Spirit upon His disciples (Acts 2.33). God promised two things;

to send the Holy Spirit to live in man again, and to baptise mankind with the Holy Spirit, just as He did the first, Adam.

The purpose of the Holy Spirit is;

1. To overcome the devil and take away the kingdom of the world from him.
2. To restore the rule/reign/dominion of mankind.
3. To restore the kingdom of God or the rulership of God back to the earth.
4. To restore the connection and the communion between God, His kingdom and mankind.
5. To transform mankind to conform to the image of Christ.

'However, when He, the Spirit of truth, has come, He will guide you into all truth; for He will not speak on His own authority, but whatever He hears He will speak and He will tell you things to come. He will glorify Me, for He will take of what is Mine and declare it to you. All things that the Father has are Mine. Therefore I said that He will take of Mine and declare it to you.'

John 16.13-15

The Holy Spirit is the God of the earth. He has been given to us by the Father (Luke 11.13). He will connect us back to heaven and bring restoration. He dwells inside of every believer, but man has to co-operate and walk with Him, otherwise the restoration will be hampered. Peter says, 'For the promise is to you and to your children and to all who are afar off as many as the Lord will call.' (Acts 2.39).

Man has become the ultimate temple (dwelling place) of the glory of God. Every true believer, anyone who is truly born of God, carries in his/her spirit the glory of God. This is the church age, the dispensation of grace, truth, and the Holy Spirit. The Holy Spirit is a gift to the church, and He is given as a guarantee. The amplified version explains it very well. 'The Spirit is the guarantee of our inheritance (the first fruits, the pledge and foretaste, the down payment on our heritage) in anticipation of its full re-demption and our acquiring (complete) possession of it – to the praise of His glory.' (Ephesians 1.14).

The glory of God is in heaven. The glory of God is in the face of Jesus Christ in heaven. The glory of God is also in the heart of man. The Holy Spirit, the Spirit of glory, who lives in us, gives us a foretaste of what is in heaven. The plan of revelation of God and His glory begins with us and within us, in this earth. We need to prepare ourselves for the Holy Spirit to manifest through us the glory of God, through Jesus Christ. 'Christ in you the hope of glory.'

There is a sacrifice to pay and the sacrifice is the crucifixion of the flesh. When you are saved or become a believer, your spirit is saved instantly but your soul is not. The soul comprises principally your mind, emotion, will, conscience and reason. This is really the heart of man, out of which comes the issues of life. The soul needs to be saved as well but it cannot be saved instantly. It is saved through a process of dying to self; crucifixion of the flesh.

'If anyone desires to come after Me, let him deny himself, and take up his cross daily, and follow Me. For whoever desires to save his life will lose it, but whoever loses his life for My sake will save it.'

Luke 9.23-24

The Holy Spirit, who is within us, will guide us into all truth so that we can be delivered from the corrupted concepts in our hearts, which control our lives and from the corrupt world in which we live. 'You shall know the truth and the truth shall make you free.'

All believers have the seed of the Spirit of glory living in them, but many of us bear no fruit of Him. The veil between our spirits and our souls is still intact. Even though the access to God is available, we cannot gain access. Jesus Christ said that 'narrow is the gate and difficult is the way which leads to life and there are few who find it.' We need to renew our minds and be transformed into the image of Christ (Romans 8.29-30). We must allow the Holy Spirit to guide us to walk in the Spirit and not to fulfil the lusts of the flesh. We should allow the Holy Spirit to lead us away from the works of the flesh (Galatians 5.17-21), into the fruit of the Spirit (Galatians 5.22-23).

Many churches have become more idolatrous than the world. Our customs and traditions have become more important to us than the voice of the Holy Spirit. We are afraid to change and have lost the spirit of revelation. We have become desensitised from the things of God, such as the world in which we live today. Where is the holiness which birthed the great revivals?

Many of us, believers, don't feel any longer any abhorrence and remorse for fornication, homosexuality, lesbianism, same-sex marriages, abortion etc. just as the world. Check the Bible, all these are abominations unto God. God hates these things. Because of these God destroyed Sodom and Gomorrah by brimstone and fire. These are some of the instruments of destruction in the end times. Yet the church is condoning these practices without telling people/nations the truth. Well, we don't want to scare them away. Perhaps the church has become more tolerant and more loving than God Himself. We are the voice of God to the nations, and it looks like we have abdicated that responsibility because of fear and persecution. The world is now leading the church.

You see, when our leaders legalise abortion, they don't realise they are releasing demonic spirits of murder into our nations and the church which should raise a voice of correction is silent. We wonder why nowadays there are murders everywhere, in our schools, on the road, even in our homes. When our leaders legalise homosexuality and same-sex marriage what they do not realise is that they are releasing demonic spirits of confusion, uncleanliness, lawlessness into our society. These demonic spirits attack our children's lives and destroy their future. The future of our nations is at stake, yet we see these abominations as hallmark of achievements in equal rights and civilization. The church should raise voices from the highest echelons so that governments would listen and take note. But if the church is not exonerated from these practices and has not positioned itself to be a voice in the wilderness, it has no voice.

Brother and sister, we are destroying the future of our own nations and bringing them under curses, and we still do not realise it. Who will plan such evil and wickedness, to destroy his/her own children and feel proud and good about it? Only the devil! The devil is using us to destroy ourselves and he may be using you. Check it! It is not the climate change that will destroy the world but sin and abominations.

Do you remember the story of Balaam? God did not allow Balaam to curse Israel. But behind the scenes Balaam taught Balak, king of the Moabites, how to get the Israelites to fornicate and therefore incur the wrath and the displeasure of God. And the plan, the doctrine of Balaam, succeeded. In the harlotry of the children of Israel with the Moabite women at Peor, the anger of the Lord was aroused against the children of Israel and 24,000 Israelites died of a plague.

The devil cannot directly defeat a true believer of Christ. But if he can entice the believer to sin and to make himself/herself abhorrence before God, he has achieved his aim. Unholiness has crept deceptively into our Christian lives and is ripe in our churches today. In the end it will destroy us and the society we live in. The atmospheres of sin and unholiness in many societies and nations have destroyed the providence and the benevolence we once enjoyed from God. Many nations are under curses and have sentenced their future children to hard and difficult battles and bondages. Christians, we need to sit up. We are being sucked into a mesh of destruction by people who do not know God. There will be weeping and gnashing of teeth in the end because we missed our time, opportunities to make things right and because we didn't realise the hour of visitation.

CHAPTER 6

Crossing The Jordan

In the last chapter we saw that the cloud of God was the symbol of God's manifest presence and His glory. The Ark of the Covenant later became the seat of the glory of God. However, the cloud rested on the tent of testimony where the Ark of the Covenant was located. When it was time to leave Mount Sinai, God spoke to Moses to make two silver trumpets and use them for calling the leaders and the children of Israel together and for directing the movement of their camp (Numbers 10.1-10). Silver is the symbol of redemption, so the use of the silver trumpets had redemptive qualities.

There were 12 tribes of Israel, and they were camped separately as for battle. Each camp would begin to move according to the sound of the trumpets. The sound of the trumpets could call the leaders or all the people to the tabernacle and could issue an alarm, or a sign to march or stop. The trumpets were also to be blown by the priests in time of war, over their sacrifices, during their appointed feasts and at the beginning of the month. The children of Israel, who left Egypt as slaves, and moved as a mob, became an organised army.

So long as the cloud remained over the encampment, the children of Israel remained where they were camped and did not journey, but whenever the cloud was taken up, they blew the trumpets and the children of Israel moved and followed the Ark of the Covenant (Numbers 9.21-23).

'Now it came to pass on the twentieth day of the second month, in the second year, that the cloud was taken up from above the tabernacle of the Testimony.

The children of Israel had stayed at Mount Sinai for about one
year. They came to Mount Sinai as disordered group of slaves
freeing from their Egyptian masters. Now the trumpets sounded, and they moved in an orderly fashion like an organised army.
The usual position of the ark of the covenant of the Lord was in
the middle of the march (Numbers 10.14-28), yet it is reported
that 'the Ark of the Covenant' went before them for a three days'
journey, to search out a resting place for them (Numbers 10.33-
34). It was indicative of the fact that the children of Israel followed
the Ark of the Covenant. Thus, they followed the glory of God.

Moses later recalled, 'So we departed from Horeb, and went
through all that great and terrible wilderness which you saw on
the way to the mountains of the Amorites, as the Lord our God
had commanded us. Then we came to Kadesh Barnea. And I said
to you, 'You have come to the mountains of the Amorites which
the Lord our God is giving you. Look, the Lord your God has
set the land before you, go up and possess it, as the Lord God of
your fathers has spoken to you, do not fear or be discouraged."
(Deuteronomy 1.19-21).

About two years after they left Egypt, the children of Israel camped
at Kadesh Barnea in the wilderness of Paran, within reach of their
promise, the land of Canaan. The promise was in sight, but instead of following the glory of the Lord as they had previously
done, their faith began to wobble.

'And the Lord spoke to Moses saying, 'Send men to spy out the
land of Canaan, which I am giving to the children of Israel; from
each tribe of their fathers you shall send a man, everyone a leader
among them.' So Moses sent them from the wilderness of Paran
according to the command of the Lord, all of them men who

were heads of the children of Israel.' (Numbers 13.1-3). However, in Moses' parting address, he indicated that the initiative to spy the land did not come from the Lord but from the people. 'And every one of you came near to me and said, 'Let us send men before us, and let them search out the land for us, and bring back word to us of the way by which we should go up, and the cities into which we shall come. The plan pleased me well; so I took twelve of your men, one from each tribe. And they departed and went up into the mountains, and came to the Valley of Eschol, and spied it out." (Deuteronomy 1.22-24).

The 12 spies returned after 40 days and reported that the land was a good land, and they brought some fruits to show it. But ten of the twelve spies also brought a bad report. 'We are not able to go up against the people, for they are stronger than we ... There we saw the giants,' (the descendants of Anak came from the giants) 'and we were like grasshoppers in our own sight, and so we were in their sight.' (Numbers 13.31-33). The children of Israel believed the bad report of the ten spies, so they murmured and complained against Moses and Aaron and refused to go and take the land of their promise. Of the 12 spies only two, Joshua and Caleb, were confident that they were able to take the land, but the children of Israel did not listen to them.

The Lord became angry with the children of Israel for their lack of faith and condemned them to a life of 40 years in the wilderness.

'For when they went up to the valley of Eschol and saw the land, they discouraged the heart of the children of Israel, so that they did not go into the land which the Lord had given them. So the Lord's anger was aroused on that day, and He swore an oath saying, 'Surely none of the men who came up from Egypt, from twenty years old and above, shall see the land of which I swore to Abraham, Isaac and Jacob, because they have not wholly followed me ...' So the Lord's anger was aroused against Israel and he made them wander in the wilderness forty years until all the generation that had done evil in the sight of the Lord was gone.'

Numbers 32.9-13

'And your sons shall be shepherds in the wilderness forty years, and bear the blunt of your infidelity, until your carcases are consumed in the wilderness. According to the number of the days in which you spied out the land, forty days, for each day you shall bear your guilt one year, namely forty years and you shall know my rejection.'
Numbers 14.33-5

The children of Israel rejected the sentence of the Lord and attempted to fight their way back into their promise, whether led by the Ark of the Covenant of the Lord or not, but they failed.

God commanded the children of Israel to turn south into the wilderness again. The children of Israel therefore stayed in the wilderness 40 years until every man 20 years of age or more who was alive in Kadesh Barnea was dead. They followed the Ark of the Covenant from Kadesh Barnea, in the wilderness of Paran, to Kadesh in the wilderness of Zin.

In Kadesh, Miriam the senior sister of Moses died and was buried (Numbers 20.1). From Kadesh in the wilderness of Zin, the children of Israel followed the Ark of the Covenant to Mount Hor, where Aaron also died. 'Then Aaron the priest went up to Mount Hor at the command of the Lord, and died there in the fortieth year after the children of Israel had come out of the land of Egypt, on the first day of the fifth month.' (Numbers 33.38). The children of Israel journeyed from Mount Hor, and after a few stops they were camped in the plains of Moab by the Jordan, across from Jericho (Numbers 33.48).

In the plains of Moab, Moses also died. 'Then Moses went up from the plains of Moab to Mount Nebo, to the top of Pisgah, which is across from Jericho. And the Lord showed him all the land of Gilead as far as Dan, all Naphtali and the land of Ephraim and Manasseh, all the land of Judah as far as the Western Sea, the South and the plain of the valley of Jericho, the city of palm trees, as far as Zoar. Then the Lord said to him, 'This is the land of which I swore to give Abraham, Isaac and Jacob saying, 'I will give it to your descendants.' I have caused you to see it with your eyes, but you shall not cross over there.' So Moses the servant of the Lord died there in the land of Moab, according to the word of the Lord. And God buried him in the valley in the land of Moab, opposite Beth Peor; but no one knows his grave to this day.' (Deuteronomy 34.1–6)

The course of this great servant of God had come to an end. He stood before the burning bush 40 years ago and stood before the greatest king in his day, the king of Egypt, to set free the children of Israel. He led the children of Israel through the Red Sea, through deserts, wildernesses, the mountains, the valleys. He had fought battles and won when there were no weapons to fight with. He had defeated giants and taken their lands. Now they were about to enter the Promised Land, but Moses was not allowed to do so because he disobeyed God at the waters of Meribah in Kadesh in the wilderness of Zin.

What did Moses do? In an earlier occurrence, when the children of Israel complained of lack of water at Rephidim, God told Moses to strike the rock that water would come out for the people to drink (Exodus 17.5–6). He did so and water came out for them to drink.

In a similar manner, when the children of Israel camped in Kadesh in the wilderness of Zin, there was no water. So the children of Israel complained and murmured against Moses and Aaron. Moses and Aaron took their concerns to God, and God told Moses, 'Take the rod; you and Aaron gather the congregation together. Speak to the rock before their eyes, and it will yield water; thus you shall bring water for them out of the rock, and give drink to the congregation and their animals.' (Numbers 20.8–9).

Moses and Aaron gathered the people before the rock. But instead of speaking to the rock, Moses spoke to the people, "Hear now, you rebels! Must we bring water for you out of the rock?'

He then lifted the rod and struck the rock twice and water came out abundantly, and the congregation and their animals drank.' (Numbers 20.10-11).

In Numbers 12.3, the Bible says, 'Now the man Moses was very humble, more than all men who were on the face of the earth.' Yet the children of Israel drove this man to anger. The Psalmist says, 'They angered him also at the waters of strife, so that it went ill with Moses on account of them; because they rebelled against his spirit so that he spoke rashly with his lips.' (Psalms 106.32-33). Moses, the humblest man on earth, lost his temper and for a brief moment disobeyed and dishonoured God.

Firstly, he spoke to the people instead of the rock. Secondly, he called the children of Israel rebels. Not that it was not true, but he was not looking at them at that moment with the eyes of God. Despite their complaints and murmurings, the loving God was supplying their need. Thirdly, he said, 'must we bring water for you out of this rock?' Moses, the most faithful servant of God turned the attention unto himself and Aaron, for a brief moment, as if they were responsible for the supply of water. They dishonoured God and did not give God the glory. Fourthly, he struck the rock twice in anger.

Water came out for the people to drink, but God was angry with Moses and Aaron. God's response was swift. 'Because you did not believe Me, to hallow Me in the eyes of the children of Israel, therefore you shall not bring the assembly into the land which I have given them.' (Numbers 20.12). Moses pleaded with the Lord to allow him to cross over. 'I pray, let me cross over and see the good land beyond the Jordan, those pleasant mountains, and Lebanon. But the Lord was angry with me on your account, and would not listen to me. So the Lord said to me, 'Enough of that! Speak no more to Me of this matter. Go up to the top of Pisgah, and lift up your eyes towards the west, the north, the south and the east; behold it with your eyes, for you shall not cross over this Jordan," (Deuteronomy 3.25-27).

Though one can sympathise with Moses, what God did was of immense prophetic significance. Moses and Aaron could not have crossed the Jordan. Their crossing of Jordan would have violated the pattern God was setting for the New Testament church. I will give you three main reasons why prophetically Moses and Aaron could not have crossed the Jordan.

1. The person who led the children of Israel across to the promise land was Joshua. The meaning of Joshua is 'Jehovah is salvation' or 'Jehovah-saved'. It has the same meaning as the name Jesus. An angel spoke to Joseph about Mary, His wife, 'She will bring forth a son and you shall call His name Jesus for He will save their people from their sins.' (Matthew 1.21). In the plains of Moab, God was laying the pattern for the change of the Old Covenant to the New Covenant; from the dispensation of the law to the dispensation of grace. Apostle Paul says clearly 'Knowing that a man is not justified by the works of the law but by faith in Jesus Christ, even we have believed in Christ Jesus, that we might be justified by faith in Christ and not by the works of the law; for by the works of the law no flesh shall be justified.' (Galatians 2.16, Romans 3.20). The law was our tutor to bring us to Christ, that we might be justified by faith (Galatians 3.24). Therefore, we conclude that a man is justified by faith apart from the deeds of the law (Romans 3.28). 'For the law was given through Moses, but grace and truth came through Jesus Christ.' It was prophetically impossible for Moses, the mediator, representing the Law, to cross Jordan into the promise of grace, represented by Jesus Christ.

2. Aaron represented the Levitical Priesthood. The Levitical Priesthood was the earthly copy of the Melchizedek Priesthood of Jesus Christ in heaven. There is no Levitical Priesthood in heaven, therefore Aaron could not have

crossed to the promise land which was the symbol of the spiritual promise of heaven. The law necessitated the order of Levitical priesthood, but the grace necessitated the order of the Melchizedek priesthood. Therefore, if perfection were through the Levitical priesthood (for under it the people received the law), what further need was there that another priest should arise according to the order of Melchizedek, and not to be called according to the order of Aaron? 'The Lord has sworn and will not relent, You are a priest forever according to the order of Melchizedek, by so much more Jesus has become a surety of better covenant ... For the law appointed high priests men who have weakness, but the word of the oath, which came after the law, appoints the son who has been perfected forever.' (Hebrews 7.11-28). The death of Aaron symbolised the spiritual change of the Levitical priesthood to give way to the Melchizedek order of priesthood in Jesus Christ.

3. The rock which Moses struck at Massah at the beginning of their 40-year wilderness experience was a symbol of Jesus Christ. 'And all drank of that spiritual drink. For they drank of that spiritual Rock that followed them, and that Rock was Christ' (1 Corinthians 10.4). So, the Rock was symbolic of Jesus Christ. 'If anyone thirsts, let him come to Me and drink.' (John 7.37). When Moses struck the rock at Massah, it was referring to the death of Jesus on the cross. 'But he was wounded for our transgression. He was bruised for our iniquity. Surely He has borne our griefs and carried our sorrows yet we esteemed Him stricken.' (Isaiah 53.4). The Bible says Jesus Christ died once for the sin of the world. 'He was taken from prison and from judgement, and who will declare His generation? For He was cut off from the land of the living; for the transgression of My people He was stricken.' (Isaiah 53.8). The Rock

had already been struck at Massah in Rephidim; symbolising the crucifixion of Jesus Christ. There was no need to strike the Rock a second time, but to speak to it in faith to receive from the stricken Rock. Jesus Christ could not be crucified twice. It was not the pattern God was laying for the New Testament church. The disobedience of Moses was therefore deeper and very serious, hitting at the very core of the plan of God. God showed His immediate disapproval, but also His love and great compassion by allowing Moses to see the Promised Land. The question I will not attempt to answer here but leave with you is this, 'With what eyes did Moses see the vast land of promise?'

So Moses died and God buried him in the plains of Moab. The plains of Moab were the last stop of the children of Israel in their wilderness experience. The wilderness was separated from the Promised Land by the waters of the Jordan. The plains of Moab were the place the children of Israel had a change of leadership and the place where Joshua and the children of Israel began to cross the Jordan into the promised land.

It looks as if Moses deliberately did not include some of the encampments of the children of Israel in the list of Numbers 33. Clearly, names like Kadesh Barnea, Beer, Mattanah, Nahallel and Bamoth were not included (Deuteronomy 1.19, Numbers 21.16-20). Kadesh Barnea should not have been left out from the list because it was the place where the children of Israel revolted against the Lord and where the anger of the Lord consigned them to 40 years in the wilderness. The total number of encampments from Rameses in Egypt to the plains of Moab, according to the book of Numbers, chapter 33, was 42.

In the genealogy of Jesus Christ in the gospel of Matthew chapter 1, Matthew also did not include all the names, but officially listed 42 generations. 'From Abraham to David, fourteen generations, from David until the captivity of Babylon, fourteen generations and from the captivity in Babylon until Christ are fourteen generations.' (Matthew 1.17). The number of stops from Rameses to the plains of Moab was 42, and the genealogy from Abraham to Jesus Christ was also 42. It suggests that each stop in the wilderness experience represented a new generation; perhaps a new problem they had to overcome or a new character/culture they needed to acquire before they could enter their promise. Each camp brought them closer to their destination, just as each generation brings us closer to the final return of our Lord, Jesus Christ, and to the millennium period.

The actual counting of the genealogy in Matthew chapter 1 shows that one generation is missing; from the captivity in Babylon to Jesus Christ is 13 generations instead of 14. There is one more stop or camp to be accounted for. There is no plausible discernible explainable for it. The last stop of Israel, the 42nd camp, was the generation of the remnant who crossed the Jordan to the promised rest or land. All the unfaithful had died in the wilderness. So, the 42nd generation in Matthew chapter 1 will be the generation of the remnant who will witness the second coming of our Lord and cross over into the millennium rest. There will have to be a 42nd generation (last generation) before the Second coming of the Lord. If we are the last generation, which I believe we are, then there is going to be a great purge of this generation so that only the remnant is left.

As the faithless children of Israel could not enter the promised land (Hebrews 3.16-19), so all the faithless Christians will not enter the millennium rest. All those who do not prepare for the coming of the Lord will be taken away by the coming affliction, persecution and/or Tribulation. There will be final tests of faith for all Christians before the return of our Lord Jesus Christ.

Israel was in the Moabite plains. Their promise was in sight, separated by the waters of Jordan. Miriam had died, Aaron had died, and Moses had died. Only the children of Israel who survived the wilderness remained. The wilderness consumed the unbelieving and the rebellious. 'For who having heard, rebelled? Indeed, was it not all who came out of Egypt, led by Moses? Now with whom was He angry forty years? Was it not with those who sinned, whose corpses fell in the wilderness? And to whom did he swear that they would not enter His rest, but to those who did not obey? So we see that they could not enter in because of unbelief. Therefore, since a promise remains of entering His rest, let us fear least any of you seem to have come short of it.' (Hebrews 3.16-4.1). The wilderness separated the obedient from the disobedient; the faithful from the unfaithful, the believing from the unbelieving. So the wilderness of our time will separate not only the believers from the non-believers, but also faithful Christians from unfaithful Christians. There must be and there will be tests of faith for people who claim to be Christians or believers.

God began to speak to Joshua after the death of Moses.

'After the death of Moses the servant of the Lord, it came to pass that the Lord spoke to Joshua, the son of Nun, Moses' assistant, saying, 'Moses My servant is dead. Now therefore, arise go over the Jordan, you and all this people, to the land which I am giving to them – the children of Israel. Every place that the sole of your foot will tread upon I have given you as I said to Moses ... No man shall be able to stand before you all the days of your life; as I was with Moses, so I will be with you. I will not leave you nor forsake you. Be strong and of good courage, for to this people you shall divide as an inheritance the land which I swore to their fathers to give them."

Joshua 1.1-6

God began for the first time to give instructions to Joshua directly, from where Moses stopped, to lead the people of Israel. The task before Joshua was very daunting and grave. The waters of the Jordan were a major obstacle to test his leadership and calling. With Moses, the children of Israel crossed the Red Sea. The obvious question was this: How was Joshua going to take the children of Israel across the Jordan? There was no other plan but to rely on God as Moses did.

The children of Israel had the law written by God kept in the Ark of the Covenant and that written by Moses at Sinai, but they also needed daily guidance from the Lord God, otherwise they would be lost and/or die. There are a lot of people who believe that all they need to know is the Bible. Sure, they need to know the Bible, but has God stopped speaking? No! The God we serve is a living God. The Bible does not tell us all about God, but gives us enough to be able to grope for Him and find Him. Without God's daily and seasonal guidance, we are all lost.

Joshua commanded the officers of the people, saying,

> *'Pass through the camp and command the people, saying, 'Prepare provisions for yourselves, for within three days you will cross over this Jordan to go in to possess the land which the Lord your God is giving you to possess.'*
>
> Joshua 1.11

This shows that the Lord God had instructed Joshua on what to do to cross the waters of Jordan. While Moses came from the tribe of Levi, meaning 'joined to', Joshua was an Ephraimite, from the tribe of Ephraim, meaning 'double fruit.' Ephraim was the second born of Joseph, but Jacob, the father of Joseph, blessed and placed Ephraim over Manasseh, the first born. "Truly his younger brother shall be greater than he, and he and his descendants shall become a multitude of nations." (Genesis 48.13–20). Jacob might have foreseen prophetically that an Ephraimite was going to lead the whole nation of Israel and divide their inheritance among them.

After the three days of preparation, the children of Israel were given further instructions.

> *'When you see the ark of the covenant of the Lord your God, and the priests, the Levites, bearing it, then you shall set out from your place and go after it. Yet there*

Joshua 3.3-5

The Hebrew word for sanctify is *'qadash.'* It means to be clean, to make clean, to hallow, to purify, to be holy or separated. It was a process of cleaning their hearts and becoming separated unto God, but it was symbolised physically by washing with water, changing clothes and refraining from sexual activity.

When they saw the Ark of the Covenant being carried by the priests towards the waters of Jordan, they followed it at a distance of about 900 metres. 900 metres was a long distance to follow for direction. It showed that the cloud and/or the fire of God's glory was clearly visible over the ark at a distance of 900 metres. They could not have followed the Ark of the Covenant without sanctification. Neither can we follow the glory of God without sanctification. The message of sanctification or holiness is very rarely addressed in our churches today. Too bad!

The Lord also said to Joshua,

Joshua 3.7-8

The baton of leadership had changed hands, but Jehovah was the same God. As He worked mighty miracles through Moses, so He worked mighty miracles through Joshua. He is the same God today, yesterday, and forever. The people would learn that He was not only the God of the past but the God of the now; a living God.

Joshua explained to his people in more detail:

Joshua 3.10-13

The Ark of the Covenant was the symbol of the glory of God, the seat of God's throne and government. The Ark of the Covenant was to be carried by the priests on their shoulders. It was usually borne on the shoulders of the children of Kohath (Numbers 4.15). Kohath was the second son (Gershon, Kohath and Merari) of Levi, the third son of Jacob. When Moses came down from Mount Sinai after the children of Israel had sinned by worshipping the golden calf, he stood at the entrance of the camp and said, 'Whoever is on the Lord's side – come to me.' And all the Levites gathered themselves together to Moses. The Levites obeyed Moses' instructions and killed about three thousand of their brothers; so God honoured the Levites and consecrated them for the work of the tabernacle (Exodus 32.26–29).

The High Priest and the priests were the descendants of Kohath. The descendants of the other two sons of Levi, the Gershonites, and the Merarites, were also used to do the work of the tabernacle; carrying the furnishings, sometimes carrying the Ark of the Covenant under supervision. In the crossing of the waters of Jordan, the Ark of the Covenant was borne by the priests themselves.

Jordan means 'descender'. The waters of Jordan began from the multiple riverbeds of Mount Hermon in the north. It descended rapidly through Lake Huleh, the Sea of Galilee, and finally into the Dead Sea in the south. Its tortuous and twisted descent of about 200 miles dropped about 3000 feet from the north to the south.

The first mention of the name 'Jordan' was in connection with Lot. There was a strife between the servants of Abraham and the servants of Lot, so Abraham advised Lot to choose the land he wanted and separate himself from him. Lot lifted his eyes and saw the plains of Jordan; that it was well watered like the Garden of Eden. Lot followed his eyes and chose the plains of Jordan, the East side of the river Jordan, for himself. God gave the west side of river Jordan to Abraham and his seed. The plains of Jordan which Lot chose turned out to be the locations of Sodom and Gomorrah, which God destroyed by brimstone and fire because of their sins.

Abram had looked after Lot like his own son. So, Lot knew the calling and promise upon Abram's life, but he decided to seek after his own self-interest. Peter called Lot a just man or a righteous man in 2 Peter 2.7, but the context was in connection with Sodom and Gomorrah. Concerning the sins of Sodom and Gomorrah, Lot was innocent, upright, and guiltless, but Lot walked by his sight and not by faith so could be considered fleshy and a man of the world.

After Lot separated himself from Abram, God said to Abram, 'Lift your eyes now and look from the place where you are – northward, southward, eastward and westward; for all the land which you see I give to you and your descendants forever.' (Genesis 13.14-15). Lot lived by sight and Abraham lived by faith. Lot could not be part of the promise of Abram, which could only be appropriated by faith.

The waters of Jordan were very important because it was the natural divide and barrier between the wilderness and the promised land. It was a symbol of the flesh, the Adamic nature. So the flesh, the old man, is a natural barrier to the things of the spirit. 'Walk in the Spirit, and you shall not fulfil the lust of the flesh. For the flesh lusts against the Spirit and the Spirit against the flesh, so that you do not do the things that you wish.'

One could only enter the promise land or the spiritual Jerusalem after passing through the wilderness and crossing the Jordan. The flesh, being our Adamic nature, can only be overcome by dying to self. So, the waters of Jordan were seen as the 'waters of death to self' or 'salvation of the soul'.

To put the admonition of Joshua in a different way, I will say, 'Look carefully, the glory of the Lord and His government is passing through the earth to your promise and rest by the way of death to self, follow the glory of the Lord carefully and respectfully because only the Holy Spirit knows the way and can guide you through it.' (John 16.13-15). For the nation of Israel it was through the waters of Jordan, but for the nation of the church it is through death to self and the flesh by the cross of Jesus Christ.

Jesus told His disciples, 'However, when He, the Spirit of truth has come, He will guide you into all truth; for He will not speak on His own authority, but whatever He hears He will speak, and He will tell you things to come.' (John 16.13). The Greek word for guide is '*hedegeo.*' It means to show the way, to be a guide or a teacher and to lead. It is the work of the Holy Spirit to show us the way through our 'waters of Jordan'.

Many Christians now think they know more about the glory of God than God Himself. Any fleshy thing that tickles their fancy they call the glory of God. The true fact is that we know nothing or very little of the glory of God. What the Bible tells us is not our reality or experience. It shows us the way and gives us a precedence that we can also participate and have our own experience. Even if we do experience the glory of God, subjectively we find it almost impossible and very difficult to describe and understand what we have experienced. The glory of God is the highest manifestation of God Himself and will definitely not conform to our earthly language, our religious practices and beliefs. In other words, we do not know the path the glory of the Lord is going to take in the near future and how and what exactly it is going to be and do. We should be very careful that we do not throw away the baby with the bathwater. We need to follow the Holy Spirit very closely to arrive at our destination and claim our promise.

> *'And as those who bore the ark came to the Jordan, and the feet of the priests who bore the ark dipped in the edge of the water (for the Jordan overflows all its banks during the whole time of harvest), that the waters which came down from the upstream stood still, and rose in a heap far away at Adam, the city that is beside Zaretan. So the waters that went down into the Sea of Arabah, the Salt Sea, failed, and were cut off; and the people crossed over opposite Jericho. Then the priest who bore the ark of the covenant of the Lord stood firm on dry ground in the midst of the Jordan; and all Israel crossed over on dry ground, until all the people had crossed completely over the Jordan.'*
>
> Joshua 3.15-17

At the time of the crossing, the Jordan was overflowing its banks and moving rapidly. It was not a good time to attempt crossing the river, but the priests carrying the Ark of the Covenant moved towards the swelling rapid waters by faith. As the feet of the priests who bore the ark touched the waters of Jordan, the waters were cut off and began to pool as far upstream as Adam. The waters to the south, to the Dead Sea, ran dry, so there were miles of dry ground before the children of Israel. Gradually about 2 to 3 million people, with their livestock and possessions, moved across on dry ground to the promised land, on the other side, opposite the city of Jericho.

The Hebrew word *'Adam'* means red or ruddy, referring to man/ mankind and the ground from which he was made from. The meaning of *'Zeratan'* is uncertain but Strong's Hebrew Dictionary suggests its root from '*tseredah*' or '*tseredathan*' which means to pierce or to puncture. The Hebrew word for 'beside' is '*tsad*.' Webster dictionary defines '*tsad*' as, at the side of, over and above, on one side and Strong Dictionary gives its figurative meaning as an adversary. So, we can deduce that before mankind can redeem his spiritual inheritance and/or enters his rest, the soul of man (flesh) must be led by the Holy Spirit through death, right from Adam on whose side was a pierce and a puncture. This Adam is no other person than Jesus Christ, the last Adam.

The picture therefore portrayed that death was rolled back to Adam by He who was pierced. It gives us a pattern that 'salvation of the soul' or 'death to self' is done through the death of Jesus Christ. Only after 'death to self' can man enter his rest or redeem his full inheritance. In other words, man can only enter his rest or inheritance through death unto resurrection of life. Death therefore is not the end but the means to the end. The Holy Spirit will take you through the cross of Jesus to your rest.

Joshua appointed 12 men and instructed them according to the Lord;

> '*Cross over before the ark of the Lord your God into the midst of the Jordan, and each one of you take up a stone on his shoulder, according to the number of the tribes of the children of Israel, that this may be a sign among you when your children ask in time to come, saying, 'What do these stones mean to you?' Then you shall answer them that the waters of the Jordan were cut off before the ark of the covenant of the Lord; when it crossed over the Jordan, the waters of the Jordan were cut off. And these stones shall be for a memorial to the children of Israel forever.'*
>
> Joshua 4.2-7

The stones were set up on the West side of Jordan at Gilgal. They were to be a sign and a memorial to future generations. The Hebrew word for sign is '*oth*,' meaning a signal, sign, beacon, or token. As a signal it pointed to Jehovah and His mighty power; as a memorial it witnessed to the miraculous crossing of the waters of Jordan.

'Then Joshua set up twelve stones in the midst of the Jordan, in the place where the feet of the priests who bore the Ark of the Covenant stood; and they are there to this day.' (Joshua 4.9). There was no command from God for another set of stones in the Jordan, so it might have been Joshua's personal witness to the crossing of the waters of Jordan.

So two sets of stones were set up. One at Gilgal (Joshua 4.19-20), where the children of Israel camped on the West side, and the other in the midst of the Jordan, in the place where the feet of the priests who bore the Ark stood on the East side.

When everything was completed, the Lord commanded Joshua, saying,

"Command the priests who bear the ark of the Testimony to come up from the Jordan ...' And it came to pass when the priests who bore the ark of the covenant of the Lord had come from the midst of the Jordan, and the soles of the priests feet touched the dry land, that the waters of the Jordan returned to their place and overflowed all its banks as before.'

Joshua 4.16-18

The priests were not just carrying the Ark of the Covenant. They were carrying the glory of the Lord, the government of God. The feet represented the authority and the dominion which flowed from the government of God. Remember, the priests themselves did not say a word, but when the glory of God moved from the waters of Jordan, it began to flow normally as before.

In the atmosphere of God's glory, His full and glorious attributes were displaced and there was no impossibility. When the glory of the Lord departed from the waters of Jordan, everything became normal again. The supernatural stopped with all its blessings. In the book of Ezekiel, the glory of God left the temple before the house of Judah was finally destroyed by the Babylonians. If anyone were left in the wilderness who did not cross the waters of

Jordan, he/she would not have entered into his/her promise and would not have survived the wilderness.

In our journey to our promise and inheritance, every person, no matter who he/she is has to cross his/her Jordan. This is God's pattern and plan. And the only one who can lead and guide us through the maze, or the wilderness of life is the Holy Spirit, the Spirit of glory. The Holy Spirit is in us, connecting us to the government of God in heaven and guiding us according to the plan and the will of God laid down from the foundation of the world. As there was a definite plan for the children of Israel of how to enter their rest so there is a definite plan for all believers to enter their inheritance.

The sound of the trumpet is sounding. It is time to prepare, sanctify ourselves for the glory of God is about to be revealed and go before us. Those who hear the trumpet and follow the glory of God will be saved and reach their destination. Those who hear this trumpet and are not prepared, like the five foolish virgins, will not go into the Millennium. Those who do not hear the trumpet are also left behind.

Perhaps we are too immersed in this world to hear the sound of the trumpet. I am not talking about the rapture or the catching up; I am talking about the call of God to begin to prepare, to sanctify yourself, to come out of the world, to renew your mind, to be transformed into the image of Christ. If you do not hear this trumpet and obey the Voice of the Advocate, the Guide, the Comforter, and the Intercessor, then you will be left behind in the wilderness of life and perish.

You cannot afford to be left in the wilderness of life or in the coming Tribulation without God's presence or the glory of God. It is time to cross the Jordan. Every believer will have to cross the Jordan for himself/herself, without that no one can enter his/her inheritance and promise. There must be a 'death to self' first.

The seed must fall into the ground and die first before it can bear fruits. No one can receive or carry resurrection life unless he/she first dies. Everyone must literally visit the cross so that the soul life can be crucified in order to release his/her spirit to be transformed to the nature and character of Jesus. This does not take a day. It is time to begin this journey and find the Way, the narrow Way (Matthew 7.14).

Many of us, while calling ourselves Christians have really made the world our reality. We honour God with our lips, but our hearts are far away from God (Matthew 7.6). Our true character and reality is of the world and flesh, conformed to it. So are many of our churches. Even many of our praise and worship songs today are not really praising and worshipping God. They point to ourselves. We have turned our churches into entertainment centres and our preaching into feel-good gospels. We mimic the glory of God with various earthly lights, smoke and fire systems. They are counterfeits to satisfy our hungry souls. As the glory of God left Judah, so the glory of God has left many churches. What is sad about this is that we do not even realise that we are missing something crucial and vital to our destiny. We need to bring back the presence and the glory of God into our lives and into our churches and remove the imitations, the counterfeits and the make-ups that have so pervaded our churches and mentality. The time we have now is very short.

CHAPTER 7

Gilgal Experiences

The children of Israel crossed the waters of Jordan on dry land into their promise land on the west side of the Jordan. God dried the waters of Jordan before their eyes and made a way for them through the waters, as He did at the Red Sea under the leadership of Moses. 'Now the people came up from the Jordan on the tenth day of the first month, and they camped in Gilgal on the east border of Jericho. And those twelve stones which they took out of the Jordan, Joshua set up in Gilgal.' (Joshua 4.19-20).

The tenth day of the first month was the day the children of Israel selected and separated their Passover lambs (Exodus 12.2-3). On that very day Israel came out of Jordan and camped in Gilgal. It was as if God had selected and separated them for a purpose. They were not the same people who were in the wilderness. They were the remnant of Israel who had passed through the river of death. So, Israel should have a new life in their promised land.

When the children of Israel began to eat the produce of the land of their promise, the manna ceased (Joshua 5.12). The exceptional favour of God they had enjoyed during their journey was over. Israel began to eat the harvest of what they sowed. Sowing and reaping, whether for good or bad, would mark their lives as matured covenant sons of God. They had to obey God's word and trust Him for the harvest.

We might have enjoyed initial blessings and favours of God as children of God. But somewhere along the line God would withdraw such favours and expect us to grow up, live by faith and follow the principles He has set for kingdom living and for victorious sons. Some of us have been children of God for over thirty years. We need to grow up and become sons of God.

The Lord said to Joshua, 'Make flint knives for yourselves, and circumcise the sons of Israel again the second time.' (Joshua 5.2). The Bible itself gave the reason why they were to be circumcised again, 'that all the men who came out of Egypt were circumcised. All of them except Joshua and Caleb had died in the wilderness but the children of Israel who were born in the wilderness during their forty-year journey were not circumcised.' Children born in the wilderness years were born into the wilderness condition, where God was the perfect source for all their needs; food, water, clothing and shelter. They never saw and did not experience the bitter slavery in Egypt. Therefore, their mind-set was different from those who died in the wilderness.

This new generation was supposed to have an unwavering faith in God. They had enjoyed the benefits of God's covenant with their fathers. Their fathers were no more. The wilderness experience was over. The new generation should cut covenant with God themselves, to be holy and to live righteously as followers of God. First, to continue to benefit from the covenant, they must become covenant and committed sons, in order to possess the promise or the land. Second, to distinguish themselves as God's people from the Canaanites. Third, their children born in the promised land must be born out of the covenant relationship with God in order to preserve the identity of the nation Israel. Joshua circumcised all the men quickly in the camp at Gilgal.

At long last the children of Israel had come to the Promised Land, after over four hundred years of waiting and forty-year journey in the wilderness. It was a time of joy and happiness. But the land of promise was already inhabited by the Canaanites. So, it was also a critical time for them to begin to learn about their new environment and think about how to defeat the Canaanites and possess the land. There were enemies all around and circumcision should have been the last thing on their minds because it would incapacitate them for some time. But God did not give them any breathing space at all. They were to take the land as covenant people who own the land and not just as people seeking a place of habitation. Their relationship with God was therefore of paramount and foremost importance. It was very important as receivers of the promise of Abraham.

'And I will establish My covenant between Me and you and your descendants after you in their generations, for an everlasting covenant, to be God to you and your descendants after you. Also I give to you and your descendants after you the land in which you are a stranger, all the land of Canaan, as an everlasting possession; and I will be their God ... As for you, you shall keep My covenant, you and your descendants after you throughout their generations. This is My covenant which you shall keep, between Me and you and your descendants after you; every male child among you shall be circumcised and you shall be circumcised in the flesh of your foreskins, and it shall be a sign of the covenant between Me and you.'
Genesis 17.7-11

It was clear that only the circumcised could inherit the Promised Land. Circumcision was the sign and the seal of the covenant between God and Abraham and his descendants. It established their relationship with God; that they were the people of God and God was their God. Circumcision was the cutting off of the outside flesh (foreskin) of the male reproduction organ. The cutting off of the foreskin was the sign of the separation from the sinful nature and fleshy lifestyle to a sanctified lifestyle (Deuteronomy 10.16, Jeremiah 4.4), so every seed of Abraham must come through circumcision. It was cut at the most sensitive and hidden place; in the heart.

Apostle Paul says, 'In Him you were also circumcised with the circumcision made without hands, by putting off the body of the sins of the flesh, by the circumcision of Christ, buried with Him in baptism, in which you also were raised with Him through faith in the working of God, who raised Him from the dead.' (Colossians

2.11-12). To the Romans, he says, 'For he is not a Jew who is one outwardly, nor is circumcision that which is outward in the flesh; but he is a Jew which is one inwardly and circumcision is that of the heart, in the Spirit, not in the letter; whose praise is not from men but from God.' (Romans 2.28-29).

The outward circumcision was the sign of an inward consecration to God. So the circumcision of the Jews in the flesh, in the Old Testament, was the type or the pattern of the circumcision of the heart of believers, in the New Testament. To the Philippians, Apostle Paul said, 'For we are the circumcision, who worship God in the Spirit, rejoice in Christ, and have no confidence in the flesh.' (Philippians 3.3).

It is not only that you are circumcised in the heart, but you are the circumcision. In the New Covenant circumcision of the heart does not occur in one day. It is a mutual continuous daily process in which man learns to yield his will to the will of the Father, through the guidance of the Holy Spirit. It changes one's mind-set to walk in the Spirit and not in the flesh. When the flesh is crucified, then man is able to worship the Father in the Spirit.

'Circumcise the sons of Israel again.' The Hebrew word, '*shub,*' translated as 'again,' means to return or turn back. Israel was to turn back to the original intent of God. To return to the original intent meant Israel was to stand at the position with God before they went to Egypt. When all circumcision was finished, the Lord spoke to Joshua, 'This day I have rolled away the reproach of Egypt from you. Therefore the name of the place is called Gilgal to this day.' (Joshua 5.9). It was as if spiritually they did not go to Egypt at all.

Circumcision was so important that the uncircumcised Israelites were not allowed to keep the Passover. 'And when a stranger dwells with you and wants to keep the Passover to the Lord, let all his males be circumcised, and then let him come near and keep it; and he shall be as a native of the land. For no uncircumcised person shall eat it.' (Exodus 12.43-48).

'Now the children of Israel camped in *Gilgal*, and kept the Passover on the fourteen day of the month at twilight on the plains of Jericho.' (Joshua 5.10). The children of Israel arrived in the plains of Jericho on the 10th of the first month, and then all the men were circumcised. On the 14th day of the same month, they kept the feast of Passover. The wounds of circumcision would have taken at least four to six days to begin to heal. But their wounds might have been healed by God in about three days to enable them to keep the feast of Passover.

To complete their journey from Egypt to Gilgal there were three Passovers. The first Passover was in Egypt. After that first Passover, they children of Israel were free to leave Egypt. They began a new life. Under the cloud of the glory of God, no one was ill, sick, weak or in any need. The Passover Lamb was a type of the crucifixion of Jesus Christ, slain from the foundation of the world. When they applied the blood to their doors, the destroyer of the Lord passed over them and killed all the firstborns of the Egyptians, but did not touch the firstborns of the children of Israel. It spoke of separation from their enemies and a mighty deliverance. Passover released them from bondage into a new life.

The second Passover was in the wilderness of Sinai, after they built the tabernacle of the Lord. It gave the children of Israel another new start in which the tabernacle worship became the centre of their lives. In that period of time, they had to follow the tabernacle and be guided by the manifest presence of God above the tabernacle and the glory of the Lord in the holy of holies.

The third Passover was in Gilgal, at the plains of Jericho and at the end of their journey. The feast of Passover in Gilgal also introduced and marked the beginning of a new life in God in which the children of Israel had to apply the principles of the kingdom for their own benefit, for their own harvest. The children of Israel in the promise land were expected to be matured son of God, knowing what to do. Passover in Gilgal would likewise invoke in them the faith of God's covenant protection and deliverance.

Each of the three celebrations of Passover opened the way for a new life and a new start; so it looked as if there was a progression into the new life of their inheritance. The first was their freedom in Egypt, a symbol of the world. The second was life after the tabernacle was built. It was Emmanuel, God with us. The third was when they reached the promise land. It was the new life of mature sons ready to take dominion. We need to take our rest before we can take possession and dominion (Hebrews 4.10).

Before the feast of Passover, the children of Israel would search their houses where they dwelt and remove every crump and trace of leaven. Israel must enter a period/feast of seven days' unleavened bread. 'And no leaven shall be seen among you in all your territory for seven days, nor shall any of the meat which you sacrifice the first day at twilight remain overnight until morning.' (Deuteronomy 16.4, Leviticus 23.6). Leaven is yeast and a symbol of sin.

A little bit of leaven, if permitted or accepted, would spread to the whole lump, the family, the church, the city or the nation. 'Therefore purge out the old leaven, that you may be a new lump, since you truly are unleavened. For indeed Christ, our Passover was sacrifice for us. Therefore let us keep the feast, not with old leaven, nor with the leaven of malice and wickedness but with the unleavened bread of sincerity and truth.' (1 Corinthians 5.7-8). It was a call to search for and remove every root of sin from their hearts and to keep their hearts pure without sin. During the feast of Passover and the feast of Unleavened Bread, Israel was symbolically free from sin.

After the Passover and the feast of unleavened bread in Gilgal, it was time to possess the promise land. Jericho was their first adversary, but Jericho was shut up, impossible to enter, physically impossible to conquer. Joshua, as the new leader, had gone by the borders of Jericho, perhaps to survey the magnitude of the problem before Israel. He lifted his eyes and 'a man stood opposite him with His sword drawn in His hand' (Joshua 5.13). He boldly went to him and asked, 'Are you for us or for our adversaries?' He replied, 'No, but as Commander of the army of the Lord I have come.' KJV uses the phrase, the 'Captain of the host of the Lord.'

Joshua immediately knew who the Captain was. So, Joshua fell on his face to the earth, 'and worshipped, and said to Him, 'What does my lord say to his servant?" Joshua was the commander of the army of Israel, but he referred to the Captain as lord, Hebrew *Adon* (lord or master), and not by the name of God. The Commander is referred to as the angel of His Presence (Isaiah 63.9), the Messenger of the Covenant (Malachi 3.1), or the angel of the Lord.

That Captain had a sword drawn in His hand, as the donkey of Balaam saw the angel of the Lord standing in its way with His drawn sword in His hand (Numbers 22.23). The Captain did not belong to Joshua, nor his enemies, but was the commander of the Lord's heavenly army. It indicated that judgement for Jericho in particular and the Amorites in general had come, and that the sins of the Amorites were full. So the battle and the conquest of Jericho and the Canaanites was not entirely in the hands of Joshua. The battle was not a physical battle, but a spiritual one. The heavenly army was there for only one purpose: to execute judgement and fulfil the plans and the will of God.

When Joshua asked what instruction the Captain had for him, the Captain replied, 'Take the sandals off your feet, for the place where you stand is holy.' It seemed to be the only answer to Joshua's request at that time. This should remind us of the encounter of Moses with the angel of the Lord in the burning bush. The Lord also told Moses, 'Do not draw near this place. Take your sandals off your feet, for the place where you stand is holy ground.' (Exodus 3.2-5).

Joshua knew that without any doubt the victory over Jericho was certain. It would have greatly encouraged him and set his mind at rest that God was in control. The Lord proceeded to give Joshua further instructions.

> 'See I have given Jericho into your hand, its king, and the mighty men of valour. You shall march around the city, all men of war; you shall go all around the city once. This you shall do six days. And seven priests shall bear seven trumpets of ram's horns before the ark. But the seventh day you shall march around the city seven times, and the priests shall blow the trumpets. It shall come to pass, when they make a long blast with the ram's horn, and when you hear the sound of the trumpet that all the people shall shout with great shout; then the wall of the city will fall down flat. And the people shall go up every man straight before him.'
>
> Joshua 6.1-5

Though the battle plan of the Lord seemed ridiculous and dangerous to any ordinary military commander, Joshua showed great faith and obeyed without any objection. The priests and the children of Israel also walked by faith and obeyed the instructions. The wilderness, the crossing of Jordan, the circumcision and the Passover had prepared their hearts for that moment.

Preparation is necessary to enter and possess our promise. 'For if Joshua had given them rest, then He would not afterward have spoken of another day. There remains therefore a rest for the people of God. For he who has entered His rest has himself also ceased from his works as God did from His. Let us therefore be diligent to enter that rest, lest anyone fall according to the same example of disobedience.' (Hebrews 4.8-11). The Greek word 'to be diligent' is *spoudazo*, meaning to labour, to speed up, to make effort, endeavour, and be diligent. It indicates that the rest/millennium and the promise of believers will not be automatic but will require some effort, labour, and diligence.

The battles before the children of Israel to possess their inheritance and enter their rest were colossal. In fact, their very lives depended on their victory. They could not win those battles by themselves, but God sent His heavenly army to fight alongside them. Likewise, the conditions of life and the battle of life just before the millennium will be unbearable, impossible to survive naturally. But God will send supernatural help from heaven to assist and support His people in order to fulfil His will and purpose.

Perhaps the greatest battle of today's Christianity is to be circumcised from the flesh and from the world. We, believers, are supposed to be the circumcision, who worship God in the Spirit and have no confidence in the flesh (Philippians 3.3), yet our greatest problem is walking in circumcision and being free from the love of the world.

We always say, we are the righteousness of Christ, but we are not walking in righteousness because we have not shed the blood of circumcision; we have not circumcised our hearts. The seed of righteousness has already been sown by Jesus Christ but it is not bearing fruit. We have rather chosen to trade on the platform of the old man, the flesh; we continue to enjoy of the tree of the knowledge of good and evil. We have chosen to trade at the gate of the devil. We are making the cross and the blood of Jesus Christ of no effect. The Bible says we should put off the 'old man' and put on the 'new man' (Ephesians 4.22-24), The second coming of our Lord, Jesus Christ, our Redeemer, is sooner than we expect, and it is time to switch and trade on the platform of the cross by shedding the blood of circumcision.

In the pattern God has given us we need to circumcise our hearts to be able to partake of the Passover and enjoy what God has for us. We have become so much engrossed with seeking the blessings of God for ourselves that our love for others have grown cold. Before Jesus left the earth, He said to His disciples, 'A new commandment I give to you, that you love one another; as I have loved you, that you also love one another. By this all will know that you are My disciples, if you have love for one another.' (John 13.34–35).

In many churches, there is so much envy, competition, rivalry, and politics which work against building a true habitation of God. We have come to serve God and mammon at the same time. We do not think about the effect of our self-centredness upon ourselves and upon the work of the kingdom. Without love all the huge ministries, their power and their achievements are nothing. 'He who does not love does not know God, for God is love.' (1 John 4.8).

Looking at the world today and the work that confronts the remnant of the *ekklesia*, especially in overcoming the enemy and bringing the souls of the world into the kingdom of God, we need heaven's assistance. The walls around us look like the walls of Jericho, closed up in apostasy, deception, ungodliness, and abominations. Many of the people of wealth and of position and of value seem to be within these walls of 'Jericho.' 'The Captain of the army of Jehovah' must visit us again. The church must begin to carry the glory of God and blow the trumpets of God and follow it if we are going to save our land and possess our inheritance.

To those who have prepared themselves in the wilderness, crossed their Jordan, truly circumcised their hearts, and are ready to overthrow the kingdom of the devil and the darkness that cover our world, the Lord will arise over them and the glory of the Lord will be seen upon them (Isaiah 60.2).

CHAPTER 8

The Glory On Mount Zion

We have seen that when the tabernacle was built at Sinai, the children of Israel began to follow the Ark of the Covenant for the rest of the journey to the promise land. They followed it into the waters of Jordan and the waters of Jordan dried before their eyes to pass through. It was due to the presence of the Ark of the Covenant that the children of Israel were able to cross the waters of Jordan into their promise land.

The first camp in the promise land was in Gilgal. It was where the tabernacle was first set up. From there, the Ark of the Covenant was used to march round the city of Jericho for seven days before Jericho fell. The tabernacle remained in Gilgal during the major part of the division of the land and was later moved and set up in a more centralised location called Shiloh. 'Now the whole congregation of the children of Israel assembled together at Shiloh, and set up the tabernacle of meeting there. And the land was subdued before them.' (Joshua 18.1). Shiloh means a place of rest. The tabernacle has come to a rest.

After the death of Joshua, the children of Israel began to fall deeper in idolatry. They worshipped carved images (Judges 18.30). Prophet Jeremiah warned the people of his day not to put their trust in the temple but amend their ways and live according to the law of God. 'But go now to My place which was in Shiloh, where I set My name at the first, and see what I did to it because of the wickedness of My people Israel.' (Jeremiah 7.12). The Hebrew word used for wickedness means bad and evil. Shiloh, the centre of the worship of God, became synonymous with wickedness and evil and God destroy the city and took the Ark of the

Covenant away. The tabernacle and the Ark of the Covenant stayed in Shiloh for over about 360 years.

At the beginning of prophet Samuel's ministry, the spiritual lives of both the children of Israel and the priesthood had deteriorated to a very low ebb. Eli was the high priest. The immorality and the debauchery of the sons of Eli had been allowed in the tabernacle services long time before them. The vile tabernacle services were a reflection of what was happening in the nation. Israel went to battle against the Philistines and things were not going well for Israel. So, Israel decided to take the Ark of the Covenant into the battle, hoping that the presence of the Ark of the Covenant would turn the tide. The Ark of the Covenant did not help them, and it was captured and taken away by the Philistines.

The sons of Eli, Hopni and Phinehas, were killed in the battle. And when Eli, the high priest, heard the news he fell off his seat and died too. Phinephas' wife was in labour; when she heard the news of her husband and the high priest, she named her child, Ichabod, meaning no glory (the glory has departed); and also died (1 Samuel 4).

The tabernacle of Moses itself escaped the capture of the Philistines but the Ark of the Covenant was taken away by the Philistines. All the sacrifices, the offerings, the ceremonies continued to take place in the tabernacle, but the Holy of Holies was empty. Ichabod! The glory of the Lord was gone. The tabernacle of Moses might have been taken back to Gilgal and then to Nob (1 Samuel 21.1). After Saul destroyed the city of Nob and killed the priests, the tabernacle was taken to Gibeon.

The Philistines who captured the Ark of the Covenant could not keep it and sent it back to Israel. The first place the Ark landed was Beth-Shemesh. The inhabitants of Bethe-Shemesh took the lid off the Ark and exposed the contents and 50,070 people died on the spot (1 Samuel 6.19). The ark was then sent to a temporary place in the house of Abinadab in Kirjath-Jearim (1 Samuel 7.1-2), before it was finally taken to Jerusalem by King David. The Ark of the Covenant was in exile for 70 years; 20 years under Samuel, 40 years under king Saul and 10 years under King David.

Seven represents fullness, perfection and completeness leading to something new. Ten is also a number for divine perfection and complete order. 70 therefore means fullness, completion of order, of law, of government, of cycle or of dispensation. After every seven is a new beginning or a resetting. And after every seventy years is a new order or a new cycle or a new dispensation. Israel was released and began to build a new temple after their seventy years captivity in Babylon.

After seventy years of the exile of the Ark of the Covenant, King David decided to bring it back to Jerusalem from Kirjath-Jearim. The first attempt failed so the Ark of the Covenant was temporary kept in the house of Obed-Edom. King David did not obey the instructions of how to transport the Ark of the Covenant and paid a price for his mistake. King David put the Ark of the Covenant on a cart, just as the Philistines had done. At the Nachon thresh-ing floor, it looked as if the ark was going to fall so Uzzah put forth his hand to steady it and the anger of the Lord was aroused and he died there by the ark.

In his second attempt, King David researched and sent the priests to carry the Ark of the Covenant on their shoulders according to the proper instructions. At that time Moses' tabernacle was in Gibeon. When David brought back the Ark of the Covenant from the house of Obed-Edom, he did not send it to Gibeon but to Mount Zion (1 Chronicles 16.1). David had pitched a tent for it there (1 Chronicles 15.1).

'David built houses for himself in the city of David; and he prepared a place for the ark of God, and pitched a tent for it.'

1 Chronicles 15.1

On Mount Zion, there was no order of priesthood and no blood and no sacrificial system. There was no established protocol on Mount Zion for approaching the Ark of the Covenant, which was the symbol of the glory of God. People could see through the tent and have a glimpse of the light of the glory of God. So, Mount Zion became a place of open heaven and the tent which David built for the Ark of the Covenant was called the tabernacle of David.

David appointed musicians to thank and to praise the Lord before the Ark of the Covenant. Before then the Ark of the Covenant was kept in the Holy of Holies and the High Priest had to prepare himself meticulously with bulls and rams before approaching it through the veil once a year on the Day of Atonement. He had to keep himself separated from everything seven days before the Day of Atonement.

In the tabernacle of David, no blood was required, no veil necessary, only thanksgiving, praise, and worship. It looked as if David was ignoring the holiness of God. It was a complete departure from the old; a new way, a new order of approaching the Most High God.

> *'So he left Asaph and his brothers before the Ark of the Covenant of the Lord to minister before the ark regularly, as every day's work required ... and Zadok the priest and his brethren the priests, before the tabernacle of the Lord at the high place that was at Gideon.'*
>
> 1 Chronicles 16.37-39

David set up two houses of worship, one at Gibeon and one on Mount Zion. He appointed two services and two high priests, Zadok in Gibeon and Abiathar at Zion. In Gibeon, in the tabernacle of Moses, they focused on the sacrificial system, the ceremonies, the feasts and the ordinances; no singing and no worship. While at Mount Zion, in the tabernacle of David, they focused on thanksgiving, praise, and worship. Thanksgiving, praise, and worship became the acceptable way of approach or access to the holy and living God.

What happened was revolutionary. Many of the Psalms were written in the tabernacle of David. 'Sing praises to God, sing praises! Sing praises to our King, sing praises!' (Psalms 47.6). 'But You are holy, enthroned in the praises of Israel.' (Psalms 22.3). 'Praise the Lord! Sing to the Lord a new song, and His praise in the assembly of saints. Let Israel rejoice in their Maker; let the children of Zion be joyful in their King. Let them praise His name with the dance; let them sing praises to Him with timbrel and harp. For the Lord takes pleasure in His people; He will beautify the humble with salvation. Let the saints be joyful in glory …' (Psalms 149.1-4).

Only God might have given David such a revelation, otherwise the result would have been catastrophic. After seventy years in exile, it was time for a new period and a new order of worship. And God allowed David to peer and tap into the time of the church age. 'But the hour is coming, and has now come, when the true worshippers will worship the Father in spirit and truth; for the Father is seeking such to worship Him.' (John 4.23). That type of approach to God existed but only in eternity where the Lamb had already been slain. I believe King David lived far beyond his time into the times of the New Testament. He could say, 'Do not cast me away from Your presence, and do not take Your Holy Spirit from me.' (Psalms 51.11), when the Holy Spirit was not even given.

'On that day I will raise up the tabernacle of David, which has fallen down, and repair its damages; I will raise up its ruins and rebuild it as in the days of old, that they may possess the remnant of Edom and all the gentiles who are called by My name, says the Lord who does this thing.'

Amos 9.11-12

Micah 4.2

The tabernacle of David is key to the manifestation of the glory of God and to the salvation of the gentiles in the end time. The gentiles would not go through the rigorous execution of the sacrificial system and the law. This pointed to the New Testament period after Jesus Christ had paid the ultimate price for sin by shedding His blood and dying on the cross. The tabernacle of David was a prophetic act. God gave to David a shadow of what was to come. In the last days, the tabernacle of David shall be raised up again and the damages and the ruins shall be repaired, so that the gentiles may come in.

King David decided and prepared himself to build a proper permanent temple for God. He received the revelation of its plan, but God chose his son, Solomon, to build it. King Solomon erected the first permanent immovable dwelling place of God. When the temple was finished, King Solomon transferred the Ark of the Covenant at Mount Zion and all the furnishings of the old tabernacle at Gibeon to the new temple. He brought together the sacrifices in Gibeon and the worship on Mount Zion under one roof.

'When the trumpeters and singers in the temple of Solomon were as one, to make one sound to be heard in praising and thanking the Lord, and when they lifted up their voice with the trumpets and cymbals and instruments of music, and praised the Lord, the temple was filled with a cloud and the glory of the Lord filled the temple.' 2 Chronicles 5.13–14

'Thus says the Lord, 'Heaven is My throne and the earth is My footstool. Where is the house that you will build Me? And where is the place of My rest?" (Isaiah 66.1). The tabernacles and the temples in the Old Testament were types of the true and final temple of God, which is man. The Jews asked Jesus for a sign and He said to them, 'Destroy this temple, and in three days I will raise it up …' but He was speaking of the temple of His body (John 2.19-21). Yes, the body of man is the true temple of God. 'Or do you not know that your body is the temple of the Holy Spirit who is in you, whom you have from God, and you are not your own?' (1 Corinthians 6.19).

Jesus again answered the Pharisees and said, 'The kingdom of God does not come with observation, nor will they say, 'See here!' or 'See there!' For indeed, the kingdom of God is within you.' (Luke 17.20-21). There is Mount Zion hidden in every born-again believer.

Jesus Christ said to the Samaritan woman,

> 'But the hour is coning, and has now come, when the true worshippers will worship the Father in spirit and truth; for the Father is seeking such to worship Him. God is Spirit, and those who worship Him must worship Him in spirit and truth.'
>
> John 4.23-24

We are the fulfilment of this prophecy, people who worship God in spirit and in truth. As we truly and sincerely worship God with a pure heart, His glory will be revealed through us on the earth. The church age itself is a preparatory stage, a rehearsal for the worship of the King of kings before His heavenly throne. At the beginning of the early church, James referred to the prophesy of Amos, in connection with the tabernacle of David.

> 'After this I will return and will rebuild the tabernacle of David, which has fallen down; I will rebuild its ruins and I will set it up; so the rest of mankind may seek the Lord, even all the Gentiles who are called by My name, says the Lord who does all these things.'
>
> Acts 15.16-17

Worship in spirit and in truth in the new covenant overshadows the old covenant approach to God through sacrifices of animals. Jesus offered Himself a sacrifice once for all time (Hebrews 7.27, 9.26). Our sacrifice is the fruit of our lips. 'Therefore by Him let us continually offer the sacrifice of praise to God that is the fruit of our lips, giving thanks to His name.' (Hebrews 13.15). This new way of approach to the most holy God paved a way for non-Jews like you and me to approach God. 'You are the chosen generation, royal priesthood, a holy nation, His own special people, that you may proclaim the praises of Him who called you out of darkness into His marvellous light.' (1 Peter 2.9).

A non-believer is like the tabernacle at Gibeon. The body-temple is present, but the glory of God is absent. But believers are like living stones chosen (1 Peter 2.5) before the foundation of the world to build the Lord God a dwelling place (Ephesians 2.20-22). When worship is truly in spirit and truth, collectively we also build God a cloud for the habitation of His glory.

Both prophet Isaiah and his contemporary prophet Micah gave an identical prophecy for the end time.

> *'Now it shall come to pass in the latter days that the mountain of the Lord's house shall be established on top of the mountains and shall be exalted above the hills and all nations shall flow to it. Many people shall come and say, 'Come, and let us go up to the mountain of the Lord, to the house of the God of Jacob; He will teach us His ways and we shall walk in His paths.' For out of Zion shall go forth the law and the word of the Lord from Jerusalem. He shall judge between the nations...'*
>
> Isaiah 2.2-4, Micah 4.1-2

> *'The Lord said to my Lord, sit at My right hand, till I make your enemies Your footstool. The Lord shall send the rod of Your strength out of Zion. Rule in the midst of Your enemies.'*
>
> Psalms 110.1-2

The above two passages show that mount Zion is not only a place of thanksgiving, praise, and worship but also the seat of God's government; where God reigns and rules. It is therefore where the throne of God is and where He makes judgements, laws, decisions, decrees, and declarations. If a believer says I decree and I declare, he/she should be very careful where he/she stands. No believer can decree and declare and have it come to pass unless the decree and the declaration has a governmental authority and power behind them. 'I decree and declare' is not just an additive to make prayers or prophesies meaningful or powerful, but an echo of God's counsel from His throne. We should be very careful, decreeing without heavenly governmental backing.

Thanksgiving, praise, and worship therefore formed the background of God's reign, rule, and governmental activities in Mount Zion. You can see why thanksgiving, praise, and worship are very important, and sometimes all that is needed for deliverance, breakthrough, and blessing. 'He is enthroned in the praises of His people.'

Now, let us try to define open heaven. A lot of churches use this phrase in their churches and programmes now. I wonder whether they are just using it ignorantly and using it to give legitimacy to what they are doing. When there is an open heaven, things are not the same again.

When the heavens opened, Ezekiel saw visions of God (Ezekiel 1.1). When the heavens opened, Jacob saw a ladder reaching the heavens from the earth. Angels were descending and ascending on it. At the top of the latter stood Jehovah and He spoke with him about future events (Genesis 28.12-13). When the heavens opened the Holy Spirit descended in bodily form like a dove on Jesus (Luke 3.21). Peter also saw the heavens open and a great sheet with all kinds of animals descended unto it (Acts 10.11-12). It was a prelude to the salvation of the gentiles. The heavens opened and Steven saw the glory of God, and Jesus standing at the right hand of God (Acts 7.55). The heavens opened and Paul encountered the Lord Jesus on the road to Damascus (Acts 9.4-5). The heavens opened and Prophet Isaiah, Prophet Ezekiel, Prophet Daniel and Apostle John all saw the throne room of God.

So what is open heaven? Open heaven is when the kingdom of heaven comes down to earth; when the veil between the heavens and the earth, between the holy place and the most holy place, between the spirit and the soul is rent asunder. When the heavens open, eternity invade time and heaven and the earth merge. It brings the kingdom of heaven, the supernatural, the reign and rule of the government of God to bear on the earth. The impossible becomes possible and natural laws are put aside to accommodate heavenly laws. When the heavens open the traffic between heaven and earth becomes busy. I like the sound of it.

I know what is going on in the mind of many. 'But the veil separating the Holy of Holies and the Holy Place was torn from top to bottom when Jesus died on the cross?' You are right. 'Then, behold, the veil of the temple was torn in two from top to bottom …' (Matthew 27.51). You see, the veil has no doors. The access is there for everybody, but one has to: One, die with Jesus on the cross to see his veil torn from top to bottom before anyone can go through. Two, one has to be declared righteous by God and pass through the flaming sword which is in the way to the tree of life. Three, one has to be transfigured into the image of Jesus Christ. Fourth, one has to smell right or have the aroma of Christ to be given access. God has only one begotten Son, Jesus Christ, and we must be conformed to His image, otherwise God does not know you. I am sorry to burst your theology.

Some of the end time prophecies or signs were the flood judgement of God, in which Noah and his family were saved because Noah was found perfect and walked with God, and the fire judgement, in which Lot and his two daughters were saved because Lot was deemed righteous, on account of Abraham, in the midst of the wicked Sodomites. Shadrach, Meshach, and Abednego were thrown into the furnace heated seven times its normal use, but not harmed. King Nebuchadnezzar saw them loosed and not hurt, walking in the midst of fire with another person like the son of God. Daniel was thrown into a den of lions, but God sent forth His angel to shut the mouth of the lions, so he was not harmed. All of the above speak of the end times phenomena and in all of them the heaven opened for them to be saved.

The days of the end times shall be horrendous and only those who will be able to walk under open heaven shall survive and become 'saviours' to other people. Walking under open heaven can be seen as the fullness of being matured sons of God. Some people, as I did myself before, have induced themselves into unpreparedness and stupor by believing that they will be raptured before Tribulation (Pre-Tribulation believers). I am sorry to disappoint you again. Your theology does not fit the pattern set by God in the Old Testament.

Walking under open heaven is likened to being on Mount Zion. Mount Zion was in southern Jerusalem, but the name 'Zion' came to represent the whole city of Jerusalem. It was where the 'tabernacle of David' was set up and where the temple of God was built.

'Then I looked, and behold, a Lamb standing on Mount Zion and with Him one hundred and forty-four thousand, having His Father's name written on their foreheads ... These are the ones who were not defiled with women, for they are virgins. These are the ones who follow the Lamb wherever He goes. These were redeemed from among men, being the firstfruits to God and the Lamb. And in their mouth was found no deceit, for they are without fault before the throne of God.'

Revelations 14.1-5, 21.1-4

The earthly Mount Zion symbolised the heavenly Mount Zion, the New Jerusalem and the holy city, the habitation of God (Psalms 74.2). It was the same city Abraham saw, believed and hoped for, which had foundation. It is the ultimate consummation of all the hopes of a believer and the end of all trials, the consummate great victory and the final place of abode, the rest.

'And it shall come to pass that he who is left in Zion and remains in Jerusalem will be called holy – everyone who is recorded among the living in Jerusalem. When the Lord has washed away the filth of the daughters of Zion, and purged the blood of Jerusalem from her midst, by the spirit of judgement and by the spirit of burning, then the Lord will create above every dwelling place on Mount Zion and above her assemblies, a cloud and the smoke by day and the shining or the flaming fire by night. For over all the glory there will be covering. And there will be a tabernacle for shade in the daytime from the heat, for a place of refuge, and for shelter from storm and rain.'

Isaiah 4.3-6

Mount Zion shall be inhabited by people whose sins are purged and who are purified and sanctified before God, and upon these the glory of the Lord shall rest. They shall be under the covering of the Lord Jesus, be protected and shall survive the oppression of the devil and also the judgement of God. They shall not escape the trials, but they shall be saved from them and the coming judgement of the ungodly.

As the Bible says, the judgement of God will begin from the house of God (1 Peter 4.17), then spread to the world. Members of the church who have made themselves ready will walk under open heaven. Jesus said, there will be wars, rumours of wars, nations will rise against nations, kingdom against kingdom, famine, pestilences, and earthquakes. He said all these are the beginning of sorrows (Matthew 24.1-7). The Greek word used for 'sorrow' means travail and birth pangs. Jesus continued to say, 'For then there will be great tribulation such as has not been since the beginning of the world until this time, no, nor ever shall be.' (Matthew 24.21).

The Old Testament prophets used the term 'the day of the Lord' to signify such a time. Prophet Zephaniah says, 'That day is a day of wrath, a day of trouble and distress, a day of devastation and desolation, a day of darkness and gloominess, a day of clouds and thick darkness, a day of trumpet and alarm against the fortified cities and against the high towers.' (Zephaniah 1.15). Prophet Joel writes, 'For the day of the Lord is coming. For it is at hand. A day darkness and gloominess. A day of clouds and thick darkness … For the day of the Lord is great and very terrible who can endure it.' (Joel 2.1-2, 11). Amos says, 'Woe to you who desire the day of the Lord! For what good is the day of the Lord to you? It will be darkness, and not light. It will be as though a man fled from a lion, and a bear met him or as though he went into the house leaned his hand on the wall and a serpent bit him! Is not the day of the Lord darkness, and not light? Is it not very dark, with no brightness in it?' (Amos 5.18-20).

Apostle Paul says, 'For you yourselves know perfectly that the day of the Lord so comes as a thief in the night. For when they say, 'Peace and safety!' then sudden destruction comes upon them, as labour pains upon a pregnant woman and they shall not escape.' (1 Thessalonians 5.2-3).

During the seven-year period of Tribulation, God will grant the antichrist, called the beast, the permission to wage war against the saints in order to test their faith. 'It was granted to him [antichrist] to make war with the saints and overcome them. And authority was given to him over every tribe, tongue and nation. All who dwell on the earth will worship him, whose names have not been written in the book of life of the Lamb slain from the foundation of the world.' (Revelations 13.7)

Another beast will arise during that period called the False Prophet who will cause all, both small and great, rich and poor, free and slave, to receive a mark on their right hand and on their forehead, and that no one may buy and sell except one who has the mark or the name of the beast or the number of his name. (Revelations 13.16-17). An angel proclaimed a warning, 'If anyone worships the beast and his image and receives his mark on his forehead or on his hand, he himself shall drink of the wine of the wrath of God which is poured out full strength into the cup of His indignation. He shall be tormented with the fire and brimstone in the presence of the holy angels and in the presence of the Lamb.' (Revelations 14.9–10).

The Greek word used for saints in Revelations 13.7 is '*hagios.*' '*Hagios*' *means holy, sanctified, or consecrated, and all 61 cases in KJV where it is used refer to believers. Revelations 13.10 reads, 'He who leads into captivity, shall go into captivity; he who kills with the sword must be killed with the sword. Here is the patience and the faith of the saints [hagios].*'

This shows clearly that some believers will be present during the great Tribulation to be tested for their faith. Apostle Paul encouraged the Thessalonians to watch, be sober and put on the breastplate of faith and love and as a helmet the hope of salvation.

> 'You are sons of light and sons of the day. We are not of the night nor of darkness. Therefore let us not sleep, as others do but let us watch and be sober. For those who sleep, sleep at night and those who get drunk are drunk at night. But let those who are of the day be sober putting on the breastplate of faith and love and as a helmet the hope of salvation. For God did not appoint us to wrath but to obtain salvation through our Lord Jesus Christ.'
>
> 1 Thessalonians 5.5-9

Many Christians have seized on the quotation of 1 Thessalonians 5.9 which says, 'God did not appoint us to wrath but to obtain salvation,' without quoting the conditions. They therefore conclude that the Tribulation is not appointed for believers. You have to be a son of light and the son of the day, and you have to be sober and put on the breastplate of faith and love and the helmet of the hope of salvation. 'For' God did not appointed us to wrath … 'For', means since, because. We fulfil the conditions because we are not appointed to wrath. In other words, if you don't fulfil the conditions the wrath will overtake you.

You see, the Greek word for wrath in both 1 Thessalonians 5.9 and Romans 5.9 is '*orge*.' '*Orge*' is defined in both the Lexical Aids to the New Testament and the Vine's Expository Dictionary as wrath in a settled and abiding condition of the mind. So 1 Thessalonians 5.9 is talking about the settled and abiding wages of sin for which we receive forgiveness and redemption through the death of Jesus on the cross. '*Orge*' points us back to the cross for forgiveness and justification.

When it comes to the end times and Tribulation, the Greek word for wrath is different. It is now '*thumos*.' 'Then one of the four living creatures gave to the seven angels seven golden bowls full of the wrath [*thumos*] of God who lives forever and ever … Then I heard a loud voice from the temple saying to the seven angels, 'Go and pour out the bowls of the wrath [*thumos*] of God on earth.'' (Revelations 15.7-16.1). *Thumos* is an expression used for a more agitated condition of wrath, an outburst or a violent motion of an inward indignation or state of the mind. *Thumos* is not translated as anger but wrath. In Revelations 16.19 where *orge* and *thumos* are used together, it is translated as the 'fiercest of His anger.'

Understanding *orge* and *thumos* shows us that God has made provision through the cross for *orge*, His anger or wrath; that we are not appointed to that type of His wrath. But when it comes to Tribulation, the Bible does not say that we are not appointed for His wrath (*thumos*). This is another blow to those who use 1 Thessalonians 5.9 as proof of Pre-Tribulation. With *thumos* God will completely destroy the present earth and heavens, end all other authorities, bring judgement to all rebellion and ungodliness, restore His righteousness, intervene directly to save His people, and pave a way for the millennium and the establishment of the kingdom of Jesus Christ.

Prophet Obadiah gives us a clue:

> '*For the day of the Lord upon all nations is near; as you have done, it shall be done to you; your reprisal shall return upon your own head. For as you drank on my holy mountain, so shall all nations drink continually; yes, they shall drink, and swallow and they shall be as though they had never been. But on Mount Zion there shall be deliverance; the house of Jacob shall possess their possessions ... Then Saviours shall come to Mount Zion to judge the mountains of Esau, and the kingdom shall be the Lord's.*'
>
> Obadiah 1.15-21

Deliverance and salvation will only be seen on Mount Zion in the terrible times of the last days. Those who have prepared themselves and dwell on Mount Zion, operating under open heaven will be saved. Prophet Obadiah uses the word 'saviours' in verse 21; plural and not singular. It shows that on Mount Zion there shall be other people who will act as 'saviours' and deliver people from the terrible times, just as Joseph did. Apart from the deliverance from Jesus Christ, there will be millions of angels, apostles, prophets and other saints in Mount Zion who will help save people in the name of Jesus.

Pharaoh changed the name of Joseph to Zaphnath-Paaneah, meaning in Coptic, the 'preserver of the age' or 'saviour.' Joseph saved Egypt and the rest of the world from a terrible famine. In the last days, the Josephs will be commissioned to supernaturally save God's people again from famine. The famine shall not only be the famine of food, but also of water, and other things like the word of God, truth, love etc. 'Behold, the days are coming,' says the Lord God, 'that I will send a famine on the land, not a famine of bread, nor a thirst for water, but of hearing the words of the Lord.' (Amos 8.11)

Prophet Joel speaking about the end time also says, 'And it shall come to pass that whoever calls on the name of the Lord shall be saved. For in Mount Zion and in Jerusalem there will be deliverance, as the Lord has said, among the remnant whom the Lord calls.' (Joel 2.32).

The Hebrew word translated as deliverance in Obadiah 1.17 and Joel 2.32 is '*peletah*,' meaning 'the escaped portion.' It refers to the remnant and not to everybody. The context of this is the end time. So prophetically, it points to the time the remnant (of the church) shall occupy Mount Zion under open heaven and operate under open access to the throne of God. This is where the salvation of the Lord will come from; this is where deliverance shall be complete and full. Those who call on the name of the Lord shall be saved on Mount Zion. In the end time God will prepare for Himself a remnant, who will walk on mount Zion, under open heaven, carrying the manifest presence and the glory of God in greater unknown measure.

The church needs to prepare the minds of the people against persecution, afflictions, oppressions, trials, travails, and those who will lose their lives for Jesus' sake. Not all believers shall survive them. Some of the believers will be martyrs. 'I saw under the altar the souls of those who had been slain for the word of God and for the testimony which they held. And they cried with a loud voice, saying how long, O Lord, holy and true, until You judge and avenge our blood on those who dwell on the earth. Then a white robe was given to each of them, and it was said to them that they should rest a little while longer, until both the number of their fellow servants and their brethren, who would be killed as they were, was completed.' (Revelations 6.9-11).

Preparing the minds of the people against persecutions, afflictions, trials, and travails and showing them the benefits of martyrdom will strengthen them when the time comes, otherwise they shall be totally unprepared, disappointed, and crushed. Many believers shall not even accept the fact that they must go through afflictions and trial because the concept of escapism has become a stronghold. The shock of unpreparedness will be enough to destroy the faith of many believers and force them to give in to defeat and to the devil.

CHAPTER 9

Coming To Mount Zion

On Mount Sinai a new nation of Israel was born, and the Old Covenant with God was constituted. Apostle Paul says, 'For you have not come to the mountain that may be touched and that burned with fire, and to blackness and darkness and tempest, and sound of a trumpet and the voice of words so that those who heard it begged that the word should not be spoken to them anymore. (For they could not endure what was commanded: 'And if so much as a beast touches the mountain, it shall be stoned or shot with and arrow.' And so terrifying was the sight that Moses said, 'I am exceedingly afraid and trembling').' (Hebrews 12.18-22).

On Mount Sinai a fearful presence of God's holiness was manifested. It was the place where the law was given at the first Pentecost. As there is no sin without the law (Romans 7.8), the law given on Mount Sinai brought sin into sharp focus. It made demands, difficult to fulfil, but offered no help. The law emphasized judgement of sin and the fear of punishment, but the law gave nothing with which to redeem mankind. The law pointed the children of Israel to a jealous God but not to a merciful and compassionate God. So, Mount Sinai gives birth to bondage and bears her children in bondage (Galatians 4.24-25).

The journey of the Ark of the Covenant, which signified the glory and the government of God, began on Mount Sinai and ended on Mount Zion. In contrast to Mount Sinai, Apostle Paul says to the Jewish believers:

'But you have come to Mount Zion and to the city of the living God, the heavenly Jerusalem, to an innumerable company of angels, to the general assembly and

First, Paul saw Mount Zion not as an earthly location but as the heavenly Jerusalem. Apostle John wrote in the book of Revelation. 'Then I, John, saw the holy city, New Jerusalem coming down out of heaven from God, prepared as bride adorned for her husband.' (Revelations 21.2).

When Paul said, "you have come to Mount Zion," he was not looking at the reality of the Christians at that time. He was looking at the end of the journey, the final and the complete picture, the rest, what every believer is promised and entitled to, of which Canaan was just a type and a symbol. What we know, and even believe, and our reality are many times completely different things. So there seems to be a journey or a process to attain what belongs to us and to be where we should be.

Paul also said, 'For if Joshua had given them rest, then He would not afterward have spoken of another day. There remains therefore a rest for the people of God.' (Hebrews 4.8-9). In Hebrews 12.1-2, Paul said, 'Therefore we also, since we are surrounded by so great a cloud of witnesses, let us lay aside every weight. And the sin which easily ensnares us and let us run with endurance the race that is set before us, looking unto Jesus, the author and the finisher of our faith.' Whether we eventually finish the race successfully depends on the type of life we have lived here on the earth.

It is possible to lose the race of life. Yes! It is a fearful thing to know that it is possible to start well and not finish your course or reach your destination successfully.

run thus: not with uncertainty. Thus I fight; not as one who beats the air. But I discipline my body and bring it into subjection, lest, when I have preached to others,
I myself should become disqualified.'

1 Corinthians 9.25-27

At the end of his earthly life Paul said, 'I have fought the good fight, I have finished the race, I have kept the faith. Finally, there is laid for me the crown of righteousness, which the Lord, the righteous Judge, will give to me on that Day, and not to me only but also to all who have loved His appearing.' (2 Timothy 4.7-8).

It is very important for all believers to know that the end of their Christian journey is crucial. The end is the deciding factor and not the beginning. 'For we have become partakers of Christ if we hold the beginning of our confidence steadfast to the end.' (Hebrews 3.14). Jesus told His disciples, 'And you will be hated by all for My name's sake. But he who endures to the end will be saved.' (Matthew 10.22). We have to remain steadfast and true, right to the end. Jesus also said, 'In My Father's house are many mansions.' The Greek for mansions, *mone*, means staying places. Heaven is just not one place but a lot of different realms and dimensions.

We may be in heaven together, but we may not stay in the same location. Where you want to be in heaven and the type of crown and reward will depending on the type of life you have lived on earth. 'Each one's work will become clear; for the Day will declare it, because it will be revealed by fire; and the fire will test each one's work, of what sort it is. If anyone's work which he has built on it endures, he will receive a reward. If anyone's work is burned he will suffer loss; but he himself will be saved, yet so as through fire.' (1 Corinthians 13-15). The person will receive nothing in heaven.

I wish I can say comfortably that all believers will make it; finish their course successfully, receive their crowns and eternally be with Jesus in the New Jerusalem. But I cannot. If it were true that once saved always saved, it would not have been necessary for Apostle Paul to discipline his body and bring it to subjection. He had to finish his race and keep his faith right to the end.

So when Paul wrote, 'You have come to Mount Zion,' he was not making a definitive statement that you are there already but, as I have explained, he is looking at the promise of the end, the complete picture; our entitlement; the sure and steadfast hope which enters the very presence of God, behind the veil, where our Lord Jesus Christ has gone ahead of us to prepare a place for the remnant and His bride. God, the Alpha and the Omega, who declares the end from the beginning, sees you at Mount Zion but where you reach there or not depends on the free-will choices you have made.

On Mount Zion, we have come to the city of the living God. There is no awesome and frightening display of God's power and glory to make us afraid and terrified as what happened on Mount Sinai. There is no consuming fire, darkness, nor tempest, nor trumpet, but we are given the Holy Spirit, not the spirit of bondage to fear, but the Spirit of adoption by whom we cry, 'Abba Father.' The Father had fulfilled His promised to give us the Holy Spirit to be with us and to dwell in us. 'The Kingdom of God is within us,' as Jesus revealed to His disciples, is an amazing revelation. Many of us have read this and believed it yet we still have no revelation of it. It is not just the knowledge and the belief but becoming one with it.

God is the same. He cannot change and has not changed since Mount Sinai, but the revelation of Him has changed. On Mount Sinai the first nation, Israel, was gripped with fear; we the second nation, the *ekklesia*, have the spirit of adoption to cry 'Abba, Father.' On Mount Zion the saints have prepared themselves and truly become one with God, true matured sons of God. Mount Zion is a gathering of God's family. 'Now, therefore, you are no longer strangers and foreigners, but fellow citizens with the saints and members of the household of God.' (Ephesians 2.19).

On Mount Zion, the curse of Eden is broken, and the cross of Jesus Christ has already dealt with sin. On mount Zion the remnant has come cleansed from sin and imputed with the righteousness of God. On Mount Zion the saints have been transformed into the image and character of Jesus Christ.

To the Colossians, Paul explained the mystery (secret) which God had hidden from both the Jews and the Gentiles. 'To them God willed to make known what are the riches of the glory of this mystery among the Gentiles which is Christ in you, the hope of glory.' (Colossians 1.27). Christ is in every believer; yet His full manifest glory is yet to be seen in their lives. The incorruptible seed of the Word which was sowed in the believer when we believed is still a seed. It has borne no fruit; it has not grown. What will give believers access to the throne room is not the gifting and what they have done, but the image and the character of Jesus Christ which they possess; the fruit of the Spirit borne in your life.

The Bible says, 'For our citizenship is in heaven, from which we also eagerly wait for the Saviour, the Lord Jesus Christ, who will transform our lowly body that it may be conformed to His glorious body, according to the working by which He is able even to subdue all thing to Himself.' (Philippians 3.20-21).

Yes, we are children of God, every born-again believer will confess that. Children are born but sons are given. A son speaks of maturity; one who behaves like his father. Every son lives to please the father. 'For as many as led by the Spirit of God, these are the sons of God.' (Romans 8.14). The great question is, 'for how long are you going to remain a child of God? When are you going to grow up and become a son?'

Sure, we can quote what the Bible says about God, which are true but are you really a son or still a child? 'Children don't differ from slaves even though they are masters.' (Galatians 4.1). Looking at what is happening in our churches today I wonder whether many of us have grown out of our spiritual childhood. Paul said to the Corinthians, 'I could not speak to you as to spiritual people but as to carnal, as to babes in Christ … for where there are envy, strife, and divisions among you, are you not carnal and behaving like mere men?' (1 Corinthians 3.1-3). Those Corinthians Paul spoke about 'fell short of no gift and eagerly waited for the revelation of Jesus Christ.' (1 Corinthians 1.8). Yet they were still babes in Christ. It is not about giftings, for these are irrevocable. It is about the type of image you bear in heaven.

Over the years Christians have developed a whole load of vocabulary that gives them false hopes and false assurances; as if they are OK, as if they have reached their destination. So the real search for a living God is put off and considered irrelevant. 'OK, the word of God is enough.' 'We don't need anything more than the word.' 'Jesus has already finished the battle.' 'All that is needed is faith.' Sure, faith is necessary, and we have to walk by faith, but when faith is not tested, when faith is without the works, it is dead. The Bible also says, 'add to your faith virtue, to virtue knowledge, to knowledge self-control, to self-control perseverance, to perseverance godliness, to godliness brotherly kindness and to brotherly kindness love, for if these things are yours and abound, you will be neither barren nor unfruitful in the knowledge of our Lord Jesus Christ, for he who lacks these things is short-sighted, even to blindness and had forgotten that he was cleansed from the old sins.' (2 Peter 15.9).

Faith indicates that there is something real, a substance. Have you seen and/or received this substance or you are still waiting and hoping? Faith gives us access to the heavenlies. Has your faith opened the supernatural door to God's presence? God intends to be found, but only by those who search diligently. You will not find Him on the surface, not on the periphery. He is the hidden treasure in the field, the beautiful pearl of great price. To find Him will cost you everything as it did to Paul. If we just follow the church's doctrines, or if we are satisfied with the present churchianity, the deceptive religious atmosphere in our churches, we shall never find God. If our churches follow the flesh and the world, God will be absent in our churches. The problem is we are not even bothered about the absence of the presence of God in our churches today. Why? Because we have substitutions, counterfeits, and are satisfied with them.

'And you will seek Me and find Me, when you search for Me with all your heart.' (Jeremiah 29.13). 'God is a rewarder of those who diligently seek Him.' They will find Him. It is time to begin to dig deeper to find God. To do that we need to re-evaluate and renew our minds from the incorrect concepts and ideologies about God which we have inherited and the centuries-old theologies which admit no new revelation. The function of the five-fold ministers must change to equip the saints to come into their inheritance and teach them to become matured sons instead of always being at the receiving end. The saints are not being led to the throne of God but dazzled with ministry gifts into perpetual dependence on the apostles, prophets, and Pastors.

Full fellowship with God is only on Mount Zion. This is where He is. This is where His Mountain is found. To emphasise this point again, it may take you through the wilderness, through the Jordan, through circumcision of your heart. You will need to follow the Spirit of Glory in your own heart to Mount Zion. Mount Zion is a heavenly location or realm where the whole family of God is present. We have been made to think that the family of God refers only to the true living believers here on earth, but according to Apostle Paul, the family of God is far greater, more grandeur and more glorious. Paul knew it because he had been there, a full conscious participant of the household of God before he physically died. According to Hebrews 12.22-24, the family comprises;

1. The living God
2. City of the living God, the heavenly Jerusalem
3. An innumerable company of angels,

4. The general assembly and the church of the first born who are registered in heaven,
5. God the Judge of all,
6. The spirits of just men made perfect.
7. Jesus, the mediator of the new covenant
8. The blood of sprinkling that speaks better things than that of Abel

The first and the Head of this family is God, described as a living God. There is only one God who is described as a living God. He is the Father, the cause and the source of life and everything in the whole universe. He is the 'I AM', the being of all things both in heaven and earth. The eternal, all sufficient, the omnipotent, omniscient, and omnipresent God, able to act and fulfil all His promises. In heaven there is no other light than the light that comes from Him. He is the 'Father of lights' (James 1.17).

The same living God is also the Chief Judge, 'God the Judge of All'. It suggests that the throne room of God is always a judicial court. God is the final arbiter of every issue and matter. And He judges according to His own righteousness, love, and holiness as a King.

Jesus Christ is the second most important family member. He is the Mediator of new covenant (Hebrews 12.24, 8.6, 9.15)), our great High Priest (Hebrews 4.14, 3.1), our Mediator, our Advocate with the Father (1 John 2.1) and our Intercessor (Hebrews 7.25). In His earthly ministry, Jesus Christ said, 'I have come as a light into the world, that whoever believes in Me should not abide in darkness.' (John 12.46). Jesus Christ came as the 'light into the world' because He is the light in heaven. The source of every light, whether spiritual or physical, is from God, the Father of lights, but it passes through Jesus Christ first. 'The city had no need of the sun or of the moon to shine in it, for the glory of God illuminates it. The Lamb is its light.' (Revelations 21.23). In other words, the whole universe is lighted by the one light, the light of Jesus Christ.

The city of the living God, the heavenly Jerusalem, is the wife of the Lamb. "Come, I will show you the bride, the Lamb's wife.' And he carried me away in the Spirit to a great and high mountain, and showed me the great city, the holy Jerusalem, descending out of heaven from God, having the glory of God. Her light was like a most precious stone, like a jasper stone, clear as crystal.' (Revelations 21.9-11).

Then there is the innumerable company of angels. Angels are ministers of God who are sometimes sent to ministers to the saints (Hebrews 1.14). They are spirits and there are as many different types and companies of angels as you can imagine. Each one has a name, is functional and has a given measure of authority. Contrary to what we have been told, all the angels in heaven are not constantly worshipping God, but there are many specialised types of work which many of these angels undertake all the time. Some may be winged but not all of them are winged. They are many angels who might look like humans and be clothed like humans (Hebrews 13.2).

'General assembly and church of the first born who are registered in heaven' refers to the church both on earth in heaven. 'There is one body and one Spirit, just as you were called in one hope of your calling.' (Ephesians 4.4). Both the church in heaven and earth must have the same function and purpose to execute the will of God. Apostle Paul says, 'We are surrounded by so great a cloud of witnesses.' This great cloud of witnesses is watching and expecting us to fulfil and complete our tasks.

'Spirits of just men made perfect' refers to both the Old and the New Testament saints who are dead. They have been declared righteous and hold eminent and special privileges and positions in heaven. Twice in the book of Revelation John fell at the feet of an 'angel' to worship him, but the angel said, 'See that you do not do that. For I am your fellow servant, and of your brethren the prophets, and those who keep the word of this book. Worship

God.' (Revelations 22.9, 19.10). John thought he was an 'angel,' but he was one of the old prophets whom God has assigned to guide and educate John.

'The blood of sprinkling that speaks better things than that of Abel' refers to the blood of Jesus. It is noteworthy to see that the blood of Jesus Christ is a member of God's family on Mount Zion. The blood of sprinkling speaks and communicates with God and with man. In heaven the blood of Jesus Christ is a form of light, just like everyone is light in heaven; so God can send the blood of sprinkling on earth as the saving light, deliverance light, purifying light, cleansing light, consuming light, covenant light, overcoming light, and many more. To plead the blood effectively is to touch a family member on Mount Zion.

Since Mount Zion is also the centre of God's government and the throne room, it can be seen with a judicial or a court room setting, with God as the Chief Judge and Jesus Christ as our Mediator and Advocate. The other six voices then become the witnesses in the courtroom that can speak on our behalf. Any of these witnesses can be used by God to help with a case before Him. Some of them may have some particular anointings and solutions to what we might be going through; some may not have completed fully their assignments and may need to complete them through us.

God can use any of the members of the family to guide, inform, protect, guard, to judge, to mediate and to bless His people. They all belong to one government, so none of them can do anything on his own outside the direction and plan of God. We also need to bear in mind that we do not worship the members of the family apart from God and Jesus Christ. We worship God and Jesus Christ and leave the administration of the kingdom in their hands. It is useless to tell God, as the King, what and how He should do in His kingdom/domain. We have become used to teaching God His job. The prophet says, 'His thoughts are not your thoughts and His ways are not your ways. For as the heavens are higher than the earth so are His ways higher than your ways and His thoughts higher than yours.' (Isaiah 55.8-9).

Some Christians label contacts with some of the family of God fake, demonic, or necromancy, but we cannot pick and choose which portions of Scripture we want and which portions we do not. The whole Bible is the word of God. It is definitely Scriptural for God to use any member of His family to fulfil a need. Elijah came back in the person of John the Baptist and will come again. At the mount of transfiguration both Moses and Elijah came back to talk to Jesus Christ about His death. It is God's government, not ours, and we must allow Him to run it the ways He wants. There is so much we can benefit if we with open minds co-operate with the other members of the family of God. I am looking forward to it myself. It is also exciting and of great comfort to learn that the Scripture speaking of the great men of faith, says, 'God having provided something better for us, that they should not be made perfect apart from us.' (Hebrews 11.40). It means some of His family members in heaven have not completed their works yet but can only complete them when they partner with us. So, as we get to the end of the age, as we are now, we are going to have many visitations from the other members of the family of God; Enoch, Noah, Abraham, Isaac, Jacob, Joseph, Moses, Joshua, David, Elijah, Smith Wigglesworth, Oral Roberts, John G Lake, Woodworth-Etter, T L Osborn, Kathryn Kulman, to name a few.

Before the end of time, all the promises, all the prophecies of God will be fulfilled. Some of the promises were started by those who have gone ahead. Some of them, in connection with the same promises, paid for them with their lives. They are watching to see it completed and they would love to lend a hand. We must look forward to such visitations and not shun it and bitterly criticise those who have such experiences.

I believe there are people who have had experiences of such visitations today but have been forced to keep quiet from sharing them because of 'false labelling'. They have decided to be careful because the very people the revelations are intended for are the same people who attack them viciously, brand them false prophets, Satanists, occultists, and witches. I could tell you experiences that would make your jaw drop, but until I receive permission from God, I feel it is better to keep them quiet.

There is no counterfeit without a reality. We need to test every spirit as to whether it is of God, as John instructs. But many of us turn to throw away everything, including what is real and true, without properly seeking the guidance of the Holy Spirit, just because we have not seen it before or because it does not rhyme with our doctrine or theology. Only the Holy Spirit has the mandate to declare what is and not of God; He alone can search the deep things of God (1 Corinthians 2.10). The Holy Spirit has not given that responsibility to any person, church, or denomination.

Some people do not believe that God has anything more to give us or teach us apart from the Bible. They deny that God still speaks apart from the Bible. They will even deny that God tests His servants before He gives them certain responsibilities. We have produced a brand of Sadducees and Pharisees in our churches more dangerous and deadly than those who lived at the time of the earthly life of Jesus Christ. Yet God has reserved the best for the last days.

Jerusalem Pentecost was just the beginning and the tip of what was to come. What we have witnessed since the beginning of the creation will be like a child play at the end of the age. The glory of God will be seven times greater in the end times to counter the seven times abomination and affliction. And God will once again use you and I, the ordinaries and nobodies. The greatest harvest is ahead of us, and the greatest move of God is before us. It is definitely something beyond what we have seen and heard so far. 'Eye has not seen, nor ear heard, nor have entered into the heart of man the things which God has prepared for those who love Him.'

CHAPTER 10

The Early Outpourings

At the first Pentecost, the glory of the Lord was manifested on Mount Sinai as a consuming fire. In the very same place God sealed a covenant with the children of Israel and the nation of Israel was born. Pentecost means the fiftieth day commemorating the events at Mount Sinai and a thanksgiving celebration of a new wheat harvest.

Pentecost was one of the seven feasts which God appointed for Israel. They were fixed times of communion and interaction with God and symbolically they portrayed the complete plan of God for mankind. Pentecost was one of the three major feasts during which all the men were required to go to the temple at Jerusalem. The other two were the feast of Unleavened Bread and the feast of Tabernacles (Deuteronomy 16.16).

The New Testament church has fulfilled the antitype of the feast of Passover and produced born again believers, fulfilled the antitype of the feast of Pentecost and birthed Spirit filled believers, but the New Testament church has not yet fulfilled the antitype of the feast of Tabernacles. The feast of Tabernacles is the last feast. It is also called the feast of harvest or the feast of the Ingathering at the end of the year (Exodus 23.16). It occurs on the fifteenth day of the seventh month of the year. The feast of Tabernacles points to the last generation and to the end time harvest of souls before the Second Coming of the Lord. It is a time of rejoicing before the Lord (Leviticus 23.40). To go through the feast of the Tabernacles is to complete God's perfect plan for mankind.

Passover was a religious celebration of the barley harvest, Pentecost a religious celebration of the wheat harvest, and Tabernacles a religious celebration of the grape harvest. Moses cautioned the children of Israel.

> *'For the land which you go to possess is not like the land of Egypt from which you have come, where you sowed your seed and watered it by foot, as a vegetation garden but the land which you cross over to possess is a land of hills and valleys, which drinks water from the rain of heaven.'*
>
> Deuteronomy 11.10-11

The land of promise of the children of Israel, which was the land of Canaan, symbolised by earthly Jerusalem, was not like the land of Egypt where they had come from. Egypt depended on the Nile, so the Hebrew slaves made irrigations and waterways and used waterwheels operated by foot to water the vegetation. They watered the vegetation themselves. The world, like Egypt, waters its own gardens by foot; by its own self effort. God had a different plan for the land of promise. In the land of promise there was no Nile. God watered the land of promise by Himself through rainfall. It was not self/human-effort but God-effort.

> *'And it shall be that if you earnestly obey My commandments which I command you today, to love the Lord your God and serve Him with all your heart and with all your soul, then I will give you the rain for the land in its season, the former rain and the latter rain, that you may gather in your grain, your new wine and your oil. And I will send grass in your fields for your livestock that you may eat and be filled.'*
>
> Deuteronomy 11.13-15 (See also Leviticus 26.1-4)

The rainfall in the promised land would be seasonal. It would also be conditional, depending on obedience to God. It was not going to be automatic. Their harvests would be preceded by two main rains, the former rain in October/November which watered, softened, and prepared the land for the seed and the latter rain in early spring, March/April, which matured and prepared the vegetation for harvest. Without obedience to God there would be no rains, and without the rains there would be no harvest. If there was no harvest, then famine and disaster would follow. So, obedience to God was crucial to the lives of the children of Israel.

In the days of Hosea, everything outwardly seemed good, prosperous and peaceful, but underneath lurked a decayed generation waiting for judgement. Does this seem familiar? A nation seemingly and outwardly fine, economically healthy, prosperous, but inside filled with decay and moral decadence. Very familiar to our western and developed nations! Hosea called the people of his day to repentance. "Come and let us return to the Lord; for He has torn, but He will bind us up. After two days He will revive us; on the third day He will raise us up, that we may live in His sight. Let us know, let us pursue the knowledge of the Lord. His going forth is established as the morning. He will come to us like the rain, like the latter and the former rain to the earth." (Hosea 6.1-3).

'Let us return to the Lord and pursue the knowledge of the Lord and He will renew our harvests. His going forth is established like the morning.' The Hebrew word for morning, 'shachar,' means dawn. Dawn is the time when light first appears in the sky before the sun rises. It is the time of revelation, refreshing and new strength. God's going forth was going to bring light and radiance, dispelling darkness, and the knowledge of the world. Secondly, God was going to come to the children of Israel like the rain; the former and the latter rains. The dawn, the new light, the new revelation of the Lord would come down like that rainfall. In other words, rainfall shall be a type of the revelation of the Lord, a type of the manifestation of His glory.

Also, in the days of the prophet Joel, a mighty plague of locusts destroyed all pasture and vegetation. It stripped the land of Judah of all green plants. The land was desolate, the streams and rivers were dry, and famine was killing both humans and animals. To Prophet Joel, it was part of the curses and the judgements Moses pronounced against those who would disobey God's word and turn away from Him (Deuteronomy 28.42). God first called the Jews to repentance. 'Turn to Me with all your heart, with fasting, with weeping and with mourning. So rend your heart and not your garments, return to the Lord your God, for He is gracious and merciful, slow to anger and of great kindness; And He relents from doing harm.' (Joel 2.12-13). The Lord was proclaiming His own name as He did to Moses when he asked to see His glory. He referred to His own divine nature of love, mercy, longsuffering, and kindness. God was giving the Jews the assurance that if they sincerely turned to Him in repentance, they would see His glory or His goodness.

Prophet Joel himself also called the people of his day to repentance, 'Blow the trumpet in Zion, consecrate a fast, call a sacred assembly; gather the people, sanctify the congregation, assemble the elders, gather the children and the nursing babes; let the bridegroom go out of his chamber and the bride from her dressing room. Let the priests who minister to the Lord weep between the porch and the altar; let them say, Spare Your people, O Lord, and do not give your heritage to reproach, that the nations should rule over them ...' (Joel 2.15-17).

The repentance was to be a very strict and a serious national repentance, involving all classes of people, from the top to the bottom. Even the priests were not exempted, nor the bridegroom. Then the Lord will be zealous for His land and pity His people. The Lord will answer and say to His people, 'Behold, I will send you grain and new wine and oil, and you will be satisfied by them; I will no longer make you a reproach among the nations. But I will remove far from you the northern army, and will drive him away into a barren land with his face towards the eastern sea ...' (Joel 2.19-20)

God called the locusts which devastated the land of Judah, the northern army. It meant the people of Judah were at war they did not realise and could not win. But God was going to remove the army from Judah and deliver His people. 'If My people who are called by My name will humble themselves and pray and seek My face, and turn from their wicked ways, then I will hear from heaven, and will forgive their sin and heal their land.' If the Jews sincerely repented and sought the face of God, He would forgive them, heal the land and restore the people.

'Be glad then, you children of Zion, and rejoice in the Lord your God; for He has given you the former rain faithfully, and He will cause the rain to come down for you – the former rain and the latter rain in the first month; the threshing floors shall be full of wheat and the vats shall overflow with new wine and oil. So I will restore to you the years that the swarming locust has eaten, the crawling locust, the consuming locust and the chewing locust, my great army which I sent among you.'

Joel 2.23-25

Prophet Joel was addressing the people of his day, but prophetically he was also addressing the nations/people of the end times and the nations/people who would turn away from God. First, there must be a sincere repentance of the whole nation, of the leaders even to the nursing babes. Without sincere and true repentance of the nation, there will be no forgiveness, and no restoration.

Many times, the sinfulness of a nation begins from the top, its leaders. In our modern world where the state is completely divorced from God, I do not see the politicians of today turning to God for answers to the problems of the land. They all pretend to have answers. They might try their best, but they always fail because the answer is found in the God they have rejected. The *ekklesia* which should lead the nations into repentance is in a mess herself. It has relinquished her voice and authority to leaders for a long time.

The response of the sincere and true repentance was that God would give the Jews the former rain faithfully; meaning the former rain and the latter rain. The devastation and the desolation of the land were so great and severe, affecting all lives, that the normal former rain and latter rain would not be able to heal the land and restore the people. It would take a great, abundant, overflowing, heavy, unusual, and extraordinary rainfall. God was going to bring a new unusual supernatural rainfall to heal the land and restore the people. This was going to be the former and the latter rain in the first month.

We can infer from the prophecies of Hosea and Joel that there will be three major rainfalls or outpourings of the Holy Spirit in the last days.

1. The former outpouring of the Spirit
2. The latter outpouring of the Spirit
3. The former and the latter outpouring in the first month

The conditions in Judah were so bad that it would be the third type of rainfall, 'the former rain and latter rain in the first month,' which would heal the land and restore the people. God would break the normal seasonal rainfall circle and introduce a new supernatural circle. The softening and the preparation of the land will be very fast; the time of sowing and maturing will also be so short that harvest will be very early and unusually plentiful. The former rain comes first and then, about six month later, the latter rain. The latter rain is normally about seven times heavier than the former rain. But in the last of these rainfalls, both the former and the latter rain will come down in one month, very fast.

Prophet Joel, right from the beginning pointed us to the end time by the expression 'the day of the Lord' as used by the Old Testament prophets to indicate the end time. 'Blow the trumpet in Zion, and sound an alarm in My holy mountain! Let all the inhabitants of the land tremble; for the day of the Lord is coming, for it is at hand.' (Joel 2.1). It suggested that the plague of the locusts was a shadow of the judgement of the end time. In other words, the end time or the last days will be a time of great famine, a time of devastation and desolation; a very gloomy and terrible time, as other prophets like Zephaniah and Amos had prophesied. But in the midst of the great devastation, desolation, and tribulation there would be the greatest and the heaviest outpouring of the glory of God, as has never been seen before, to heal the land, restore the people and bring in greatest harvest of souls.

Prophet Amos saw this glorious restoration when the ploughman would overtake the reaper. 'Behold, the days are coming, says the Lord, when the ploughman shall overtake the reaper and the treader of grapes him who sows seed. The mountains shall drip with sweet wine and all the hills shall flow with it.' (Amos 9.13). He is talking about the grape harvest, which is the feast of the Tabernacles, the last feast on God's calendar, indicating that it will occur in the last days. The time between sowing and reaping will be very short. Judgements will come more quickly than we are normally used to, and harvest will be quick, plentiful, and abundant, unlike anything we have seen in the past. Time will generally seem shorter and faster.

Prophet Joel continued, 'You shall eat in plenty and be satisfied, and praise the name of the Lord your God, who has dealt wondrously with you; and My people shall never be put to shame. Then you shall know that I am in the midst of Israel; I am the Lord your God and there is no other. My people shall never be put to shame.' (Joel 2.26-27). God would heal the land and restore the people for His own name's sake.

We have seen that rainfall is a type or a shadow of the outpouring of the Spirit of God, which is also the outpouring of the glory of God. So we conclude from the prophecy of Joel that in the last days there will be the greatest and mightiest outpouring of the Spirit of God such as the world has never seen before. The harvest of souls will be unbelievably greater and faster because of the heavy outpouring of the glory of God. There will be no period of time in comparison to the end time in connection with harvest.

Prophet Joel prophetically foresaw the outpouring of the Spirit of God in the last days:

'And it shall come to pass afterward that I will pour out My Spirit on all flesh your sons and daughters shall prophesy, your old men shall dream dreams, and your

Joel 2.28-29

In the Old Testament the Holy Spirit came only upon priests, kings, and prophets chosen to do the work of God. But a time was coming when Spirit of God would be poured on all flesh, even on servants. There would be no distinction due to race, colour, nationality or age. 'Your sons and daughters shall prophesy, your old men shall dream dreams and young men shall see visions'. Dreams and visions are all aspects of the prophetic. So, a time would come when ordinary people would be prophetic, having the ability to know the will and the mind of God. The prophetic will be the dominant gift in the last days.

The outpouring of the Holy Spirit could only be a New Testament experience. There was no rain of fire or the outpouring of the Holy Spirit in the Old Testament. It would have consumed the recipients. God, the Father baptised Jesus Christ with the Holy Spirit at the waters of Jordan, as our example. But after the redemption of mankind through the death, resurrection and ascension of Jesus Christ, the way was open for the outpouring of the Holy Spirit to fall on mankind again. John the Baptist said, 'I indeed baptised you with water … He (Jesus) shall baptize you with the Holy Spirit and fire.' (Mark 1.8, Matthew 3.11).

Jesus Christ, Himself, told His disciples to wait for it. 'Behold I send the Promise of My Father upon you; but tarry in the city of Jerusalem until you are endued with power from on high.' (Luke 24.49). After Jesus resurrected from the dead, He first breathed the Holy Spirit into His disciples just as to the first Adam. 'Receive the Holy Spirit.' (John 20.22). But the disciples still had to wait for the enduement of power before they could start their ministries. To 'tarry' is to sit down or to set, to enthrone, to wait and to be 'endued' is to sink into, to be clothed or to be vested.

Jesus was referred to the baptism in the Holy Spirit, which occurred at the Jerusalem Pentecost, as a 'vestment' or 'clothes of power.' The disciples were to wait to be vested, clothed, or enthroned with power from above. The Greek word used for 'power' in this verse (Luke 24.49) is '*dunamis*.' '*Dunamis*' is inherent power, ability, miraculous working power. The baptism in the Holy Spirit could not happen while Jesus Christ was alive because a covenant was to be enacted, which of necessity required the shedding of blood.

'For where there is a testament, there must also of necessity be the death of the testator. For a testament is in force after men are dead, since it has no power at all while the testator lives.'

Hebrews 9.16-17

Jesus was the covenant maker, the Testator. For 40 days after His resurrection, Jesus taught His disciples about the kingdom of God. When they asked Him about the restoration of the kingdom of Israel, Jesus replied, 'It is not for you to know times or seasons which the Father has put in His own authority. But you shall receive power when the Holy Spirit has come upon you; and you shall be witnesses to Me in Jerusalem and in all Judea and Samaria, and to the end of the earth.' (Acts 1.6–8). The same inherent miraculous working power, *dunamis*, is used here.

10 days after Jesus' ascension to heaven, making it exactly 50 days after His resurrection, while His disciples waited with one accord, they were baptised in the Holy Spirit and with Fire.

'When the day of Pentecost had fully come, they were all with one accord in one place. And suddenly there came a sound from heaven, as of a rushing mighty wind, and it filled the whole house where they were sitting. Then there appeared to them divided tongues, as of fire, and one sat upon each of them. And they were all filled with the Holy Spirit and began to speak with other tongues, as the Spirit gave them utterance.'

Acts 2.1-4

First, it happened 50 days after resurrection, precisely at the feast of Pentecost, because it was the antitype to the Old Testament Pentecost at Mount Sinai. Second, the disciples were with one accord in one place. They were not divided in their minds, mission, or purpose. Jesus had told them to wait in Jerusalem for the enduement of power and they were praying/waiting for it, sitting down. There was going to be a form of enthronement.

Third, suddenly there came a sound from heaven. It sounded like a rushing mighty wind and filled the house. Every sound has its frequency and wavelength. The sound was not an earthly sound but a heavenly sound. Heaven was announcing its presence. The sound filled the house and changed the natural atmosphere of the place where they had gathered into a heavenly atmosphere. It means the disciples were first emerged or baptised into the atmosphere of heaven before being baptised into the Holy Spirit. They switched realms, from the natural to the heavenly.

Fourth, 'there appeared to them divided tongues, as of fire, and one sat upon each of them.' They were baptised into fire. The heavenly fire purified and consecrated them, enthroned them, and then empowered them. The holiness of God at Mount Sinai manifested as a consuming fire, so fiercely that the children of Israel were afraid and stood far off. And here at the Jerusalem Pentecost the disciples were baptised in the holy Fire without any harm. They were purified, consecrated, and took on the characteristic of the image of Christ and the fire anointing so they could operate with the fire anointing. The Greek word for baptism is *'baptizo' which means to be dipped, immersed, covered or enveloped; so it was not a little tongue of fire on top of the disciples, but a big flame which covered and enveloped them.*

Fifth 'they were filled with the Holy Spirit.' Wherever there is the fire of God, there is also His presence. The Holy Spirit is the third Person of the Godhead. He is the executive arm of the Father. And He is the God who is with us on the earth. Jesus told

His disciples, 'But when the Helper comes, whom I shall send to you from the Father, the Spirit of truth who proceeds from the Father, He will testify of Me.' (John 15.26). 'However, when He, the Spirit of truth, has come, He will guide you into all truth; for He will not speak on His own authority, but whatever He hears He will speak; and He will tell you things to come. He will glorify Me, for He will take of what is Mine and declare it to you. All things that the Father has are Mine. Therefore I said that He will take of Mine and declare it to you.' (John 14.26, John 16.13-15).

The Greek word used for the Holy Spirit is *'parakletos.' And it is translated as* Intercessor, Helper, Advocate, Counsellor, Comforter, Strengthener, and Standby. He is the One Summoned, one called to one's side. Jesus also said, 'I will pray to the Father, and He will give you another Helper, that He may abide with you forever.' (John 14.16). The Greek word for 'another' is *'allos.' According to the Lexical Aids to the New Testament, it means 'another' numerically, but of the same kind. They are different Persons, yet the same kind; so the Holy Spirit will continue the work of Jesus Christ on the earth.*

'Nevertheless I tell you the truth. It is to your advantage that I go away; for if I do not go away, the Helper will not come to you; but if I depart, I will send Him to you.' (John 16.7). The Holy Spirit has been re-sent by the Father through Jesus Christ and will be here on earth until all the work of the Father is done. He is the Father's representative on Earth and we should not underestimate His importance in the world.

Sixth, they began to speak in other tongues. Baptism of the Holy Spirit is also the sign of our salvation and speaking in other tongues is the outward visible expression of that sign. Speaking in other tongues is an indication that one has been baptised into the Holy Spirit. When we speak in other tongues, we are expressing the fact that we are purchased by Jesus' blood, belong to Jesus Christ, and have the Holy Spirit living in us. Therefore, speaking in other tongues can be a powerful declaration and powerful voice or tool against the forces of darkness.

Speaking in tongues is also one of the ways God has given us to edify our spirits. 'He who speaks in a tongue edifies himself …' (1Cor 14.4). The Greek word to 'edify', '*oikodomeo*,' comes from two words, '*oikos*' meaning 'a house' and '*domeo*' meaning 'to build.' So, to edify, *oikodomeo*, means to build a house/temple or to restore/rebuild a house/temple. Speaking in tongues can be a powerful means of building or rebuilding our bodies, our churches and/or nations. In Jude verse twenty, Jude said, 'But you, beloved, building yourselves up on your most holy faith, praying in the Holy Spirit.' (Jude 1.20). The Greek word for building is '*epoikodomeo*.' Here the Greek word '*epi*' is added to the word *oikodomeo*. *Epi* means upon. So, 'building' here means building upon a house. Every born–again believer is a house/temple, has a foundation (which is Christ) and a measure of faith (Romans 12.3). One of the ways of building upon ones' foundation and faith is to cultivate a lifestyle of speaking in tongues.

At the Jerusalem Pentecost, the Jews had gathered in Jerusalem from many nations. When the disciples were baptised in the Holy Spirit and began to speak in other tongues, the multitude came together, and was confused. They heard the disciples of Jesus speaking in their own languages. Then they were all amazed and marvelled, saying to one another. 'Look, are not all these who speak Galileans? And how is it that we hear each in our own language in which we were born? … We hear them speaking in our own tongues the wonderful works of God. So they were all amazed and perplexed, saying to one another, 'Whatever could this mean?' Others mockingly said, 'They are full of new wine.'

But Peter, standing up with the eleven, raised his voice and said to them:

'Men of Judea and all who dwell in Jerusalem, let this be known to you, and heed my words. For these are not drunk, as you suppose, since it is only the third hour of the day but this is what was spoken by the prophet Joel: 'And it shall come to pass in the last days, says God, that I will pour out of My Spirit on all flesh; your

Acts 2.17

Peter declared that what was happening was the fulfilment of the prophecy of Joel. It was only the third hour outpouring of the Holy Spirit; meaning there were two more to come; the sixth hour and the ninth hour. Three outpourings of the Spirit of God. Prophet Joel said, 'And it shall come afterward,' but Peter said, 'And it shall come to pass in the last days.' Peter was implying that the last days had begun. It was the first outpouring of the Holy Spirit or the former rain. The cloud of glory in heaven broke and it rained fire. Being the first and the former rain, it was to water, soften the hearts of people and prepare their hearts for the seed, the gospel. Pentecost was also a wheat harvest and therefore those gathered in and those who received the word and were baptised on that day were about three thousand (Acts 2.41).

Peter speaking about the outpouring at the Jerusalem Pentecost said, 'Therefore being exalted to the right hand of God, and having received from the Father the promise of the Holy Spirit. He poured out this which you now see and hear.' (Acts 2.33). Jesus received the promise of the Holy Spirit from the Father and poured Him upon them. For three and half years Jesus trained the 12 disciples, now they were ready. He told them, 'As the Father has sent Me, I also send you.'

It is very important to emphasise that the Holy Spirit did not baptise the disciples once and for all. The fire of the Holy Spirit came upon them over and over again and they were filled with the Holy Spirit again and again. Peter was filled with the Holy Spirit on the day of Pentecost but when the disciples faced the Sanhedrin the Bible says, in Acts 4.8, 'Then Peter, filled with the Holy Spirit, said to them, 'Rulers of the people and elders of Israel…by the name of Jesus Christ of Nazareth whom you crucified, whom God raised from the dead, by Him this man stands here before you whole." The disciples were filled again with the Holy Spirit when they prayed for boldness in the face of affliction. 'And when they had prayed, the place where they were assembled together was shaken; and they were all filled with the Holy Spirit, and they spoke the word of God with boldness.' (Acts 4.31). The outpouring or the infilling or the falling of the Holy Spirit brought the experience of the manifest presence of God and the baptism of fire along with it.

Apostle Paul was not one of the 12 apostles of Jesus Christ, but Paul had an encounter with the risen Lord on the Damascus road and was filled with the Holy Spirit when Ananias prayed for him (Acts 9.17). Paul always referred to himself as an apostle of Jesus Christ. In Acts 13.9, Paul was filled again with the Holy Spirit when he confronted Elymas the sorcerer. In Acts 13.52, both Paul and Barnabas were filled again with the Holy Spirit in the face of persecution.

These subsequent infillings restored the original individual fires. Anytime the apostles needed flesh power, anointing or wisdom to accomplish the work of the kingdom, they were filled again; the fire would fall again. The infillings were tailored to their needs and circumstances. Anytime they faced flesh obstacles or the powers of darkness and they relied on God, they were filled with the Holy Spirit again and the fire of God would come upon them again. In other words, they would be re-vested/re-clothed with power from above. Those infillings and fire revivals were usually accompanied by various miracles, signs, and wonders. It was never self, mental knowledge, theology, the usual method, or the know-how. It was always the infillings from above. The disciples could not have done the work of God without the infilling and the anointing of fire.

Many of us today, when we are baptised in the Holy Spirit, think it is done; that is it. But it is not the case at all. Holy Spirit should come upon us over and over again. We should continually be in prayer and cultivate the presence of the Holy Spirit. Baptism in the Holy Spirit virtually opens the heavens and releases supernatural gifts and supernatural enablement in specific areas.

Baptism in the Holy Spirit quickened the spirits of the apostles to access the spiritual realms. By so doing they were able to bring down the reign and rule of God, thus establishing the kingdom of heaven on earth. The apostles preached and pointed people to the King and His kingdom, and signs and wonders followed their ministry. The fire confirmed their callings and empowered them to fulfil their callings. We need the fire.

Immediately after the Jerusalem Pentecost, a man lame from his mother's womb was healed by Peter and John at the gate of the temple. Peter said, "Silver and gold I do not have but what I do have I give you. In the name of Jesus Christ of Nazareth, rise up and walk.' And he took him by the right hand and lifted him up, and immediately his feet and ankle bones received strength.' Peter said, 'What I do have I give to you.' Both Jesus and Peter had passed the same man several times, but at the particular time Peter knew he had something within him to give to the lame. Peter felt the stirring of the deposit or the enduement of power welling in him. All the people who saw the miracle were filled with wonder and amazement at what had happened.

God formed Adam from the dust of the ground. He breathed into his nostrils the breath of life and Adam became a living soul. The Spirit of God dwelt in Adam and so he was connected directly to God. When Adam sinned in the Garden of Eden, the Holy Spirit left, and Adam spiritually died. He was cut off from God. The Holy Spirit had to leave because the fire of His glory would have destroyed Adam. God drove Adam out of the Garden of Eden and placed cherubim at the east of the Garden of Eden and flaming swords which turned every way to guard the way to the tree of life.

The tree of life was a symbol of eternal life. 'And this is eternal life, they may know You, the only true God and Jesus Christ whom You have sent.' The Greek word 'to know' is *'ginosko,'* *which means to know experientially, not intuitively or mentally. It therefore speaks of an intimate relationship between the person knowing and the object of knowing. In this intimate relationship, one is changed from glory to glory (2 Corinthians 3.28) until the two become one. To know God is to become one with God. The tree of life also becomes the symbol of God.*

If Adam had been allowed to eat of the tree of life, Adam would have lived eternally in sin and would have made redemption impossible for him and for mankind. It would not have been necessary for Jesus Christ to come to the earth to redeem mankind.

Many Christian believers know about God and about Jesus Christ mentally. They know what the Bible says about them, and perhaps believe in them. That is good. But they have been made to believe it is enough. No, that is not enough at all. It is like reading a book and believing that you personally know the writer. No, you do not. God is a person, and many Christians do not know Him even though they know about Him. To know Him experientially is to have a real, living intimate fellowship with Him.

The way to such a relationship was guarded by cherubim who oversee the glory of God and the flaming sword. The flaming sword is a ball of fire which we must pass through to eternal life. The descendants of Adam (mankind) remained outside of the Garden in Eden until the day that the sin of Adam was paid for by Jesus Christ. 'But God demonstrated His own love towards us, in that while we were still sinners Christ died for us. Much more then, having now been justified by His blood, we shall be saved from wrath through Him.' (Romans 5.8-9). To be justified is to be declared innocent. 'In Him we have redemption through His blood, the forgiveness of sins, according to the riches of His grace.' (Ephesians 1.7). Redemption means to ransom in full or to pay/buy back.

When the full price of redemption was paid by Jesus Christ; man was declared innocent through the blood of Jesus. Therefore, the access to the garden in Eden and the tree of life reopened through Jesus Christ. The flaming sword would still block the path to the tree of life, but once one is born again, purified by holy fire and declared innocent, he/she is able to pass through the flaming sword without any harm. The flaming sword will not destroy the person.

At the Jerusalem Pentecost when the tongues of fire fell on the one hundred and twenty disciples and nothing happened to them, it was a sign that they were already redeemed and declared innocent. The Holy Spirit had come back to live in man again (John 14.16-17, 1 Corinthians 6.9). Alleluia!

Before Jesus Christ ascended to Heaven he commanded his apostles to go and make disciples of all men. 'And they went out and preached everywhere, the Lord working with them and confirming the word through the accompanying signs.' (Mark 16.20). The close relationship with the risen Lord continued even when they were baptised in the Holy Spirit and endued with power from on high, so their ministries were attended with great power and great grace (Acts 4.33).

There were mighty miracles in the days of the early apostles; like the lame at the beautiful gate (Acts 3.4-5). There were public mass healings and deliverances (Acts 8.6-7, 16.16-23). Even the shadow of Peter would cause the sick to be healed and the bed-ridden to be made whole (Acts 5.15). Multitudes of the sick and those tormented by unclean spirits were all healed (Acts 5.16). Angels became very active in their ministries. The angels helped and worked together with the disciples (Acts 5.19-20, 8.26, 12.5-11, 27.23). People were raised from the dead (Acts 9.40, 20.9-10). Philip was translocated from the Gaza road to Azotus (Acts 8.39-40) in a moment, a distance of over 30 miles.

Even though each of the apostles of Jesus had mighty gifts, they walked and worked with the risen Lord personally and were not solely dependent on their gifts. That was the greatest difference between the apostles of Jesus and many of our church leaders today. Many of us do not know

As mighty as the deeds and the miracles of the apostles of Jesus
Christ were, they were the beginning of the last days and a partial fulfilment of the plan of God. It was only the third hour
outpouring, the former rain. There would also come the 'latter
rain' and the 'former and the latter rain in the first month' as we
have earlier discussed. The last rain or the last outpouring of the
Holy Spirit would be far, far greater than the former or the latter rain. I cannot begin to imagine the greatness, the splendour,
and the majesty of the glory of God that is about to manifest in
this last generation.

It is therefore very difficult to imagine what is going to happen
in the last outpouring of the Spirit of God. I believe some of us
present today will be part of the last generation, so we should be
open-minded to the last outpouring of the glory of God otherwise we shall miss it and/or not recognise it. It may not be what
we are used to or what we are expecting.

The Jerusalem Pentecost started with the Jews, but it later began
to fall/rain also upon the Gentiles. Apart from Paul, who was very
learned when he first received the baptism of the Holy Spirit, the
rest of the early apostles of Jesus Christ were ordinary men, who
were filled with power and operated under open heaven. They
walked with the Lord, not only physically but spiritually. Each
of them was called to a different ministry. They dispersed and
travelled to most of the principal cities of the world at that time,

places we know today as Rome, Syria, Turkey, Ethiopia, Arabia, India, Persia, Russia, and Tunisia. All of them, apart from John, the writer of the book of Revelation, died as martyrs in the first century. The blood they shed became seeds for the foundation and the growth of the true gospel of Jesus Christ and the end time church that will overcome the whole world and finish the race.

At the first Church Council in Jerusalem, James quoted the prophecy of Amos to support Apostle Paul and Barnabas that it was not necessary for the Gentiles to be circumcised and keep the Law of Moses. 'After this I will return and will rebuild the tabernacle of David, which has fallen down; I will rebuild its ruins and I will set it up; so that the rest of mankind may seek the Lord, even the Gentiles who are called by My name, says the Lord who does all these things.' (Acts 15.16–17).

We have seen that Jesus Christ fulfilled the tabernacle of David. The tabernacle of David needed to be rebuilt and restored in our day. Jesus came not to destroy the old covenant but to fulfil it. Many churches of today operate like the temple in Gibeon. The services are going on alright, but the manifest presence and the glory of God are absent. Even much of what we call worship is just good music or counterfeits with no fruit of the presence of God. Could it be one of the reasons why we are not able to fulfil the mandate of the great commission today? Many of our 'holy services' are just 'man–made services.' We need to rebuild and restore the tabernacle of David.

As the antitype of the Sinai Pentecost, the Jerusalem Pentecost was the original intent and the substance of God's plan (Colossians 2.17) from which all the shadows, patterns and types took their forms, so Jerusalem Pentecost cannot be seen as a revival. It was also not a restoration or an awakening. It was the establishment of the God's original plan.

If we look at the Old Testament types, we see that in our world today all spirit filled believers have spiritually passed through

Passover and camped at Mount Sinai. This is the time of Pentecost. In other words, the church is camped at Pentecost, but the greatest tragedy is that it has camped there permanently and is not prepared and ready to move. Just as the children of Israel could not engage with the presence of God on Mount Sinai, the church camped at Pentecost cannot intimately engage with the presence of God. The glory of God was at Mount Sinai, yet Israel worshipped the golden calf; so churches today with all the blessings of Pentecost are worshipping the golden calves of our day. To move from Pentecost is very essential and crucial. But to move from Pentecost, that is 'Mount Sinai,' is to go through the wilderness until we cross the Jordan, enter the promise, and come to Mount Zion. The trouble is, we don't want to move from Pentecost. We are proud to be called Pentecostals but afraid of the real fire of God.

Many of our church leaders and members have not experienced the wilderness yet. Many have not crossed the Jordan yet. We have made the church so fluffy that it has no substance; full of leaves but no fruit, full of smoke but very little fire. It looks naturally good, but it is spiritually infantile. We speak charismatic tongues but there is no fire in it; there is no real power. The old Pentecostals would have been shocked, because to them the baptism in the Holy Spirit was accompanied with sanctification, genuine conversion, baptism of fire and power. Many people are born again but not converted. Christianity has become just intellectual and traditional. Their real heart-life has nothing to do with Christ.

Many of us pastors, prophets, apostles, and bishops preach and minister to the people but we have not really encountered the Lord Jesus. Many of us, to be frank, have very powerful giftings and we have taken them as the end of all; all that is to it. Many of us massage our giftings and/or commercialise our giftings to advertise ourselves for gain. Many of us don't even realise the offices have time limit, that offices would give way to something higher, greater and new.

We have not learnt to wait on the Lord, we cannot wait. Perhaps it is the culture of our time. In the realms of heaven, we need to wait. Many young pastors of today are in a hurry. They have not been processed, they are half-baked, and they want to reach the top of their ministry in a very short time. You can see a lot of them on the social media. They mean well, but still repackage the same unfruitful messages without God's life. No wonder some of our church leaders have gone for the power of darkness to help them to operate. This is preposterous and sounds unreal, but it is at everywhere we turn. We just want the vain glory, the wealth and the accolades that come with power. Since when did God seek help from the devil? Many 'Christians' in those churches, just looking for signs and wonders, are deceived, unknowingly lost and doomed.

Many of us who are supposed to be leaders have not learnt to walk daily with the Lord Jesus. We use only our theological knowledge and experience to do the work of God. Many of us have focused mainly on the things the people want to hear and have failed to announce to them what God is saying. As such we have failed or failing to prepare the people for the second coming of the Lord. It might be that we do not really hear the Voice of God ourselves. We have lifted our eyes off the glory of God unto the glory of man and the world, so our churches have become centres of the world. Even the worst vile happenings in the world are found in our churches today. We have failed to lead the world to the truth. The world now is leading the church to its doom.

We need the baptism of fire today. We need the glory of the Lord in our time. We need to repair the damages and the ruins of the tabernacle of David. The challenges we face in this last generation are such that we need the fullness of the Holy Spirit. The generation in which we live is unique. We need extraordinary and unique demonstration of God's power to do the work. Many of us are doing something which seems good for the kingdom but way out of the plan of God. The church has acquired a language of self-delusional half-truths and motivational language, perhaps to make believers feel good inside. We sow a whole lot of religious false-truths, which stop our spiritual process. Successive generations have repackaged the old mistakes. These false-truths or half-truths have been so reinforced with time that they are set in our minds as the truth. There is very little acceptance of new revelations. We are happy with false prophets and we pursue the true prophets of God and hound them out into silence. Father help us.

The world has moved on, now well baked and strengthened in its apostasy and hardened against the word of God. But the church has not moved on. We are using the old tools of 50-70 years for today's generation. The old evangelistic methods will no longer work today. We need the seasonal manifest presence of God to help us in the time we are in. We need the help of angels, of the glorified saints who are watching and praying for us. We need to turn to the 'powers of the age to come.' They have been there in their infancy, now we need them in their fullness. The glory of the latter church must be greater than the former. The 'former rain and the later rain must come in one month' to bring restoration in our time.

CHAPTER 11

Through The Second Outpouring

The first New Testament outpouring of the Spirit of God, the Jerusalem Pentecost, was the anti-type of the manifestation of the glory of God at Mount Sinai. At the first outpouring the apostles and some disciples of Jesus Christ were baptised in the Holy Spirit and fire. It endued them with power to carry forward the ministry of Jesus Christ. At the same outpouring, the church as a body was born and the apostles of Jesus became the first leaders. In a short time, about 60 to 70 years, the gospel of the kingdom had spread throughout the then world.

The church in Jerusalem initially suffered great persecution from Judaism, so they were scattered to other regions including Samaria. Then Peter preached the gospel to Cornelius' house, and they also received the gospel. Gradually through the ministry of Paul, Barnabas, and others the gospel reached almost all the major cities of the world (at that time) within 60 to 70 years. The next great persecution came from the Imperial Roman Empire, the most powerful empire in the world. By the 2nd century AD all the apostles of Jesus Christ, except John, had been martyred in different parts of the world. In the 3rd century AD, a Roman general, Diocletian, seized power and became the emperor of Rome. He divided the Imperial Rome into the Eastern Empire, governed from Byzantium (later called Constantinople), and the Western empire, governed from Rome.

In the 4th century AD, Constantine the Great succeeded his father, Constantius Chlorus, who was Caesar (deputy emperor) in the Western Roman Empire. Constantine was politically married to the daughter of the emperor at that time, Augustus Maxentius.

Constantine the Great fought for control and in 312 AD defeated Augustus Maxentius to become the emperor of the Western Roman Empire.

Before the battle, it was claimed that Constantine had a prophetic vision in which Jesus told him to re-paint all the shields of his warriors with the overlay of Greek letters X and P (which at that time was the symbol of Christ) and he would win the battle. When he did that and won the battle, he claimed conversion to Christianity from paganism.

In 313 AD Constantine, the western Roman Emperor, signed an edict in Milan with the eastern Roman emperor Licinius to stop the persecution of Christians. The edict legally granted religious freedom of worship to all people throughout the empire, and so the official persecution and martyrdom of Christians which began with the first apostles came to an end. The initial conversion of Constantine might have been only partial. He was a sun worshipper before his conversion, so he syncretised the sun worship with Christianity. He was however baptised a Christian on his death bed in 337 AD.

With the edict of Milan in 313 AD, Christianity began to be the dominant religion in Rome. Constantine convened the first council of the Christian church in Nicaea in 325AD to address doctrinal issues and to formulate one belief structure for the church. It resulted in the adoption of the Nicene Creed as the official statement of faith for Christians. In 380AD, Emperor Theodosius I revised the Nicene Creed and made Christianity the official religion of Imperial Rome, to the exclusion of all other religion.

Rome refused to acknowledge the headship of the Jerusalem church with James, the brother of Jesus, as its first Bishop. Rome stopped the election of Jewish Bishops and elected its own non-Jewish Bishops and leaders. The Bishop of Rome was called the Pope. The Pope was the Holy Father, the Vicar of Christ, the Supreme

Pontiff, His Holiness. The name seemed later to merge with the office of the emperor of Rome. Because of Imperial Rome, the church in Rome became the Roman Catholic Church and spread to all her colonies.

The Roman Catholic Church took upon herself the right to punish those who refused to become her members – not much for religious freedom. It changed most of the Jewish traditions and forced its own religious traditions on the people. Those who refused to comply were punished, some by imprisonment and others executed. The Roman Catholic Church assumed the power to confiscate the property and the wealth of those it considered to be 'opponents' or 'heretics.' It arrogated to itself the power to absolve people from sin on payment of money. It also saw itself as having the power to overwrite God's word by its own man-made rules and enforce them on people.

Constantine's first Sunday law in 321 AD played a major part in the final change of the Sabbath from Saturday to Sunday (the day of the sun god). The Imperial Roman Catholic Church validated Constantine's change from a Saturday Sabbath in favour of a Sunday Sabbath. The first celebration of the birth of Christ on the 25th December occurred under the emperorship of Constantine. He allegedly collaborated with the Roman Catholic Church to mark 25th December as the birthday of Jesus. 25th December was the official celebration of the birthday of the sun god, 'Sol Invictus' (unconquerable sun) in the later Roman Empire. These and many changes were made to shift the church from the Jewish root and merge it with paganism in Rome so that the church would appeal to pagans (and all under the rule of the Roman Empire).

Apostle Paul says the church was grafted unto the Jewish stem (Romans 11.15-19). The Jewish nation was really the first church, therefore their traditions formed the initial structures and oracles upon which God interacted with mankind. The Jews laid the foundation of the knowledge of the true God, the priesthood, and the glory of God. By removing the Jewish roots and traditions the church began to function without proper foundation. The way was then open to inculcate the Roman polytheist and pagan cultures into Christianity; thus, the true gospel of Jesus Christ was officially greatly compromised, impoverished and adulterated, giving rise to various abuses and excesses in the church.

The decline of the Western Roman Empire marked the beginning of the Dark Ages (Middle Ages) and also the decline of the political, economic, and cultural strength of the empire. That period, from the 5th century to the 15th century, was also a dark period so far as the church was concerned. The Roman Catholic Church continued to be prominent, but the Church's doctrines and practices were corrupted and influenced by political, economic, and financial considerations. The true gospel of Jesus Christ was almost non-existent.

The eastern Roman Empire, the Byzantine Empire, continued to survive after the decline of the Western Roman Empire, but in the 7th century the eastern Roman Empire was overrun by an Islamic Caliphate. Crusades, mounted by the Western Christians, tried to regain control of the holy land but failed. The Byzantine Empire finally fell to the Ottoman Empire in 1453 AD.

There was a need to restore the original fire that prepared the ground for the gospel and empowered the apostles of Jesus Christ for the work of the ministry. There was a need to revive the church. 'Revive' comes from two words; *'re' which means 'again' and 'vive' meaning 'to live'. So, to 'revive' means to live again, to bring back to life and vitality, to rekindle and to restore life to something which is dead; in this case the church.*

Early meaning of the word Revival had been a seasonal outpouring of the Holy Spirit to empower, awaken and restore the dying, lethargic, and backslidden churches and Christians. Revival was not initially for the non-Christians. You cannot revive where life had not been or rekindle where there had never been a fire. Those revived became convicted of sin; encounter the love, the righteousness, and the holiness of God in a new way. They became more spiritually awakened, more spiritually sensitive, had more power to do God's work and more zeal for the ministry of the gospel. There was a transformation in their hearts that affected their whole lives. The revivals also prepared the hearts of non-Christians to receive the gospel and become Christians. So, in revivals, the backslidden returned with greater zeal and many souls were won for the kingdom of God as a result of that.

Revival is a sovereign act and a move of God and can never be scheduled. We pray for it, but it comes from God. It could occur suddenly and unexpectedly and can affect churches, cities, and communities at God's will. Nobody knows exactly when it would come. Over the years people have used the word 'revival' to refer to evangelistic meetings and crusades, unusual phenomena of the Holy Spirit, theological movements, and social reforms. It may not be easy, therefore, to define revival to cover every use of the word today. My main concern of revival here will be limited to the outpouring of the Holy Spirit that transforms lives, prepares hearts for the harvest of souls and the actual harvesting of souls for the kingdom of God. We have to take note that before and after these revivals, there would usually be various drizzles and ripples of varying intensities here and there, and historians label them differently. But according to Prophet Hosea and Prophet Joel, there will be only three major rainfalls or outpourings of the Holy Spirit before the end of the church age.

After the first outpouring of the Holy Spirit in Jerusalem and the passing away of the early apostles, the Holy Spirit seemed to have been silent, especially in the dark ages. At the close of the dark ages, Martin Luther (1483-1546), a German monk, rejected and repudiated several doctrines and practices of the Roman Catholic Church and led a protestant Reformation. Martin Luther translated the Bible into German and taught that the Bible was the only source of divine revelation containing all things necessary for salvation and sanctification through faith. The Bible translation into German began to put the Bible into the hands of ordinary people instead of the Roman Catholic priests alone. A split between the Roman Catholic Church and those who opposed her doctrines and practices became inevitable. The Protestantism came out of that split. The Protestant Church itself later split into many doctrinal groups, e.g. Lutherans, Quakers, and Pentecostals.

The real spiritual foundation of the church had been corrupted and polluted by the Roman Catholic Church, so the overall direction of the early apostolic church was thwarted, or diverted, and misrepresented. Even though the Protestant Church broke away from Roman Catholic Church, some philosophy of the Protestant church continued to draw its strength from the Roman Catholic Church's philosophy.

Signs of revival began to be seen in the 18th century through the ministries of certain people such as Jonathan Edwards, an American Calvinist theologian and preacher, John Wesley, a British clergyman and itinerant preacher. The ministry of John Wesley saw a noticeable outpouring of the Holy Spirit. Multitudes were convicted of sin and came to the Lord. In the ministry of John Wesley, the Holy Spirit would suddenly fall upon people to such an extent that they would show outward signs of His presence. John Wesley started a new denomination, called Methodism, which spread to other nations, such as America. George Whitefield, another British clergyman, had a similar ministry in the American colonies.

The late 18th century to early 19th century saw people like Charles Grandison Finney, American Presbyterian minister, whose meetings were filled with signs and wonders. The population of towns was said to have increased by two-thirds during those periods and crimes were alleged to have dropped by two-thirds during his time. In the late 19th century an American itinerant woman evangelist called Maria Woodworth-Etter (1844-1924) came to the scene. Her meetings were evidently attended with the outpouring of the Holy Spirit. People would run to the altar crying for repentance; others would fall down under the power of God. Later in her meetings there were miracles, healings, and trances. Thousands of people were healed and converted. She might have been the forerunner of Pentecostalism.

The beginning of the 20th century saw the Welsh Revival and the Azusa Street Revival. The Welsh Revival began in the late 1904 under the leadership of a 26-year-old former collier and a minister in training, called Evan Roberts. He felt the need to depend more on the Holy Spirit. In one of his prayer meetings the Holy Spirit descended with great power upon the people, and people began to cry, praise God, and pray as never before. That outpouring continued for less than a year but, in that short period of time, it was estimated that about 100,000 souls were converted and came to the Lord.

The Welsh Revival spread from place to place where people gathered to pray for revival: in Scotland, in England and in Ireland. Churches were filled across the whole denominational spectrum. Drunkards, prostitutes, and the rejects were transformed. It is also estimated that in less than 2 years more than 5 million people were converted to the Lord. News of the Welsh Revival reached Europe, Canada, and America and empowered Christians to pray for the outpouring of the Holy Spirit.

The Azusa Street Revival was led by William J Seymour, a black American of slave descent, born in 1870. He was initially tutored by an American preacher/tutor called Charles Fox Parham who believed in the baptism of the Holy Spirit with the evidence of speaking in tongues. William Seymour began to preach the baptism of the Holy Spirit by faith even though he had not received the baptism in the Holy Spirit. In Los Angeles, when he began to preach about the baptism of the Holy Spirit, he was locked out of the church which had invited him. He began to hold prayer meetings in a private house in Bonnie Brae house. Then suddenly in 1906 the fire of the Holy Spirit began to fall upon those in the prayer meeting and baptised them in the Holy Spirit with the evidence of speaking in other tongues. A powerful outpouring of the Holy Spirit followed, and many received the baptism of the Holy Spirit with the evidence of speaking in other tongues, including William

Seymour himself. Soon Bonnie Brae house became too small, so they moved to 312 Azusa Street.

In Azusa Street the fire of God would fall during the services and people would fall under the power of God. At that time falling under the power of God was not as common as we know it today. The fire of God was so strong and unusual that people literally saw fire on top of the building. People walking past the building and those living blocks away came under conviction and some were slain in the Spirit. The outpouring of the fire of the Holy Spirit came with phenomenal creative miracles. Missing legs, missing arms, missing eyes were recreated and restored. Many other incredible miracles took place before the eyes of the people present. Services were round the clock, so the doors of 312 Azusa Street were not closed. News of the Revival spread all over the world. For over three years the revival continued, day and night and people came all over the world to receive baptism in the Holy Spirit, anointing and many other blessings and gifts of the Holy Spirit.

Baptism in the Holy Spirit spread all over the world through Pastors and other ministers who had gone to the Azusa Street Revival. In Azusa Street Revival the fire of Pentecost came back in a mighty way and birthed forth a tongue speaking church. There had never been such a mass baptism in the Holy Spirit since the Jerusalem Pentecost. In the Azusa Street Revival, white and black people were mixed together under the same roof – there was no segregation. Sadly, within the leadership in Azusa Street brewed a concoction of disagreements, misunderstandings, doctrinal differences, selfishness, and other unchristian behaviours. By 1909, the original leaders had been reduced to a few to carry on the work. It was not the same Azusa Street Revival as before, but continued until about 1915.

No revival was recorded just before and after the First World War, but after the Second World War there arose some well-known evangelical and Healing Revivalists, led by people such people as T S Osborne, Billy Graham, Jack Coe, A. A. Allen, John J. Lake, William Branham, Smith Wigglesworth, Aimee Semple Mcpherson, Oral Roberts, Reinhardt Bonke, and Benson Idahosa. Those evangelical meetings and Healing revivals, I believe were part of the waves of the Pentecostal fire. They touched the world with the power of God and multitude of people all over the world came to the Lord. Another great healing Evangelist was Kathryn Kulman, an American itinerant evangelist whose ministry became well known in the late 1940s. She conducted healing meetings in America and round the world. What was unique about her ministry from the rest of the other healing evangelists was that she did not lay hands on people for their healing. People were healed while in the service, even while in their seats. She laid great emphasis on the Person of the Holy Spirit and her meetings were saturated with the Presence of the Holy Spirit. She might have been the bridge to the coming Charismatic movement.

In the 1960s came the Charismatic Movement, an outgrowth of Pentecostalism. It became an interdenominational Christian movement which believed that a born-again Christian has to be baptised in the Holy Spirit with the evidence of speaking in other tongues. Charismatic Christians believe the gifts of the Holy Spirit are for today, including laying on of hands. Charismatic Christians normally have exuberant church meetings. It is one of the most popular Christian movements today. But the fire which accompanied Pentecostal encounters in both the Jerusalem Pentecost and Asuza Street Revival seems to be absent.

Charismatics also tend to lose the sense of the holiness of God and the need for sanctification. They emphasise the gifts of the Holy Spirit to the exclusion of the fruit of the Holy Spirit. The emphasis of the doctrine of holiness and sanctification which catalysed revivals in the 18th and 19th centuries is obviously absent in our churches today. So long as people are praying in other tongues and having the gifts of the Holy Spirit, they believe they are alright with God. It is a false concept. The Corinthian church was not deficient in the gifts of the Holy Spirit, but Paul called them babes (1 Corinthians 3.1-3).

The outpouring of the Holy Spirit or revival is sometimes also referred to as a Visitation, Move of the Holy Spirit or a Move of God. There were three main outpourings that had affected the world since the first Outpouring, which we have called the Jerusalem Pentecost; the Wesleyan Outpouring, sometimes referred to as the First Awakening, in the 18th century, which birthed the Holiness Movement; the Welsh Revival, which birthed prayer movements for the outpouring of the Holy Spirit in many countries; and the Azusa Street Revival, which birthed the Pentecostal Revival in the early 20th century. I believe that the Wesleyan Outpouring began to revive the church after about 16 centuries of persecution, controversies, abuse, lethargy, and fruitlessness. The Welsh Revival was the immediate precursor to the Azusa Street Revival and therefore prepared the ground for that move of God. I seem to agree with those who see Azusa Street Revival as the latter rain; the second major Outpouring of the Holy Spirit.

The Latter Rain, the Pentecostal Revival, gave rise to the Evangelical Revival, Healing Revival and the Charismatic Revival or Renewal. The Charismatic Renewal pioneered the restoration of the gifts of the Holy Spirit and the endorsement of the fivefold ministry gifts, especially the prophets in the 1980s and the apostles in the 1990s. The Prophets and the Apostles were needed to rebuild the church and to bring order, discipline, and direction to the church. But this work has not been properly done, as the church is still in a mess.

The church has commercialised and prostituted the gifts of the Holy Spirit and franchised them. There are so many abuses and counterfeits of the gifts of the Holy Spirit that some people shy away them or reject them altogether. The Charismatic Revival which propelled the church forward from the 1960s seems to be fading out. Many churches and ministers have become stuck with the gifts of the Holy Spirit to the exclusion of the fruit of the Spirit. Our mind-set is locked on Pentecost as if there is nothing more God will or can do. Perhaps it has become our comfort zone, where there is very little or no accountability. As the pattern in the Old Testament indicated, the Pentecost at Mount Sinai was never meant to be the final camping ground or the final destination of the children of Israel.

About a year after the Pentecost at Mount Sinai, God told the children of Israel to begin to move to the promised land. 'Then the Lord said to Moses, 'Depart and go up from here, you and the people whom you have brought out of the land of Egypt, to the land of which I swore to Abraham, Isaac and Jacob, saying, 'To your descendants I will give it'' (Exodus 33.1). The final destination so far as the glory of God was concerned was Mount Zion. Mount Zion is the place of open heaven. It is the place where the heavens and the earth merged into one.

To camp permanently at Mount Sinai or at Pentecost is suicide in the end times, because the glory of God will move from Mount Sinai, away from Pentecost, to different camp sites. Once you are left behind at Mount Sinai you cannot survive. You will die with only the powers of Pentecost. In the end times Jesus Christ is going to use people who have moved from the feast of Pentecost to the feast of the Tabernacles. Those who have crossed the 'waters of Jordan' and camped on Mount Zion, the last stop, will be operating under open heaven and will be part of and see the glory of the later temple and the 'powers of the age to come.' The 'powers of the age to come' are powers the majority of which have never been fully revealed here on earth. These are the special unknown powers that are going to be manifested in the last days.

While praying, the Spirit of God spoke these words into my spirit: 'limousine-driven church.' A limousine is a long luxurious car usually driven by a chauffeur who is separated from the passengers by a partition. People hire such limousines for occasions such as weddings and special celebrations.

While meditating on what the Spirit said, it occurred to me that these limousine-driven churches are mainly being driven by flashy and ostentatious ambitions, something that is meant to impress people. These are like flashes in a pan. They are attempts to portray an outward well-being, but inwardly these churches are fleshy and can be described as whitewashed sepulchres. They do not have true spiritual influence and dominion. Such churches have lost their light. They are no longer effective. A lot of activities, a lot of programmes, but they only function in the soulish realm and fleshy platforms. They do not seem to connect to the manifest presence or to the throne of God. They can only connect to people of their kind but not to the real sons of God.

The chauffeurs of these limousine-driven churches are cut off from the people they minister to because they have cut themselves off from the living God. I do not mean going to a Bible school, knowing the Bible or even preaching from the Bible. I mean going to the secret place where God truly is, his throne room, and having such intimacy with God that He reveals His mind and His heart to them. Many believe that the fact that they are preaching from the Bible is enough. Is it really?

When one hires a limousine, he/she tells the driver where he/she wants to go. Many members of the church believe their Pastors are leading them to God or to heaven. But the fact is that the Pastors, the Apostles, the Bishops cannot lead you where they have not been. So where are they leading the flock to? If they never have a living experience or encounter with the living God, how can they lead the flock to also have a living experience and encounter with God? How are they really going to help the flock achieve their life's goals, when these goals are written and stored in God's presence? It would look as if the pastor, the Apostle, the Prophet, or the Bishop is leading the congregation, but the true fact is that the congregation is directing the leadership of the church what they want to hear and where they really want to go. The congregation becomes the light of the Pastor and the leader.

Jesus told His disciples "They are blind leaders of the blind. And if the blind leads the blind, both will fall into a ditch." He told the Scribes and the Pharisees, 'Woe to you Scribes and Pharisees, hypocrites! For you shut up the kingdom of heaven against men; for you neither go in yourselves, nor do you allow those who are entering to go in … you travel land and sea to win one proselyte, and when he is won, you make him twice as much a son of hell as yourselves.' (Matthew 23.13-15).

For many centuries we have been handed down some teachings and theological beliefs that do not really help us have experiential knowledge of God. Knowing the word of God or preaching the word of God alone is good but not enough. We must experience what is written in the Bible. James says, 'But be doers of the word, and not hearers only, deceiving yourselves.' (James 1.22). And Paul says, 'The letter kills but the Spirit gives life.' (2 Corinthians 3.5-6).

Many Christians are deceived because they are born again, baptised in water, and baptised in the Holy Spirit, and they have been made to think that is all there is to it. 'I am the righteousness of God' and 'I have a relationship with Christ.' 'Alleluia, I am going to heaven.' Well said! But what is our reality? Are all these words our reality or just what we have picked up from the church or from the Bible without understanding them?

What sort of relationship do you have with God? Do you really know the Person of God? Many of us know about Him; we read the Bible and have heard hundreds of messages about God, but still do not know Him, because we have blocked our own minds from going any further. The fact is when you are born again and baptised in the Holy Spirit, your training has just begun.

Many of us believe that there is no need for any further training or schooling in the pursuit of God. God is a good Father, far, far better than an earthly father. Having children is great, but every father wants sons who are intimate with him and whom he can depend and rely on and trust. Every father trains his children to be matured. And God is no exception.

The church has become so fleshy, fluffy, and merged with the world and humanistic doctrines and agenda that it seems to have become an extension of the world. It should not be so. The church largely seeks to please the world instead of pleasing God. The Church is the chosen generation; chosen out of the world; a royal priesthood and a holy nation (1 Peter 2.9). The word church, translated from Greek, *ekklesia*, means an assembly of people called out from. The Bible says clearly that whoever will be a friend of the world is an enemy of God (James 4.4).

The time of the message/service has been cut short in order that people will not grumble. Our style of worship has become more fashionable. It seeks to entertain rather than lead people into God's presence. Many of our worship songs do not focus our minds on God but upon who we are, what we want, and where we want to be and go. We say the songs reflect the current culture. If we are the righteousness of God, why don't our worship songs reflect it? We seek more to entertain people and be more social minded than God minded. Very few people attend prayer meetings and Bible studies.

The modern-day church has become more of a seeker-friendly church and lost her voice and power. In order to woo people into the church and/or prevent them from leaving, the church has compromised the truth of the gospel. Out go messages of the blood of Jesus, messages about sin, the need for repentance, deliverance, sanctification, self-control, and death to self. We dare not mention things like alcoholism, fornication, and homosexuality in church services. All we think about is what we can get from God. Seeking and pursuing of prosperity has deadened our spiritual senses and destroyed our ability to seek and pursue God for who He is.

Many believers of our day only want to hear messages that seem to bring blessings, exaltation, and provision. God really blesses, exalts, and provides. These are the offshoots of our relationship with God. But many believers have put them first before God. They want to walk in the flesh, receive the best of the world, and at the same time receive the best in heaven. They want to walk in sin and disobedience and still enjoy the pleasures of heaven. They want to reap where they have not sowed. They want to serve God and mammon at the same time. Needlessly they shout Amen, Alleluia, glory, to any declaration that will fancy their selfish hearts, but they have really closed their hearts and minds to the truth. Many do not want to hear other parts of the Bible which bring repentance, correction, chastisement, sacrifice, giving, self-denial, and obedience. Touching on these topics brings a sudden quietness in the church. 'For the time will come when they will not endure sound doctrine but according to their own desires, because they have itching ears, they will heap up for themselves teachers and they will turn their ears away from the truth, and be turned aside to fables.' (2 Timothy 4.3-4). This time is with us now. People move from church to church, not seeking the truth, but where their itching ears will be tickled and their souls elated.

I have been an ordained minister of the gospel for over 30 years, and I do not need anybody to tell me that the church is in a serious mess. If anyone is open-minded he can see that things are not working well in the church. Things are not moving forward. Things are not moving the way God intended them to move. We still look back at the early witnesses and graces of the church. If Prophet Moses were here; if Apostle Peter were here, if Apostle Paul were here. We have not been taught to see that the times we are in are the best times; when the full glory of God can be revealed.

Anybody gets up and calls himself/herself Pastor, Bishop, Apostle, Major Prophet, the Most Eminent Excellent Prophet etc. We seem to take pride in titles. A minister said to me that if I wanted a new title, he could arrange for it for a fee. I said no; God has not told me to do that. So long as we have a religious title, we become bloated and untouchable. Who is going to question when someone who calls himself a prophet says, 'Thus says the Lord' – whether it is true or false cannot be easily challenged. At the end of the day the innocent is deceived and pay a big price.

We teach people to conform to our churches, but we do not teach them to be transformed into the glory and the image of Christ. Perhaps many of our church leaders are not transformed into Christ's image themselves. That is why we see a lot of them advertising themselves and their gifts. 'Let this mind be in you which was also in Christ Jesus, who, being in the form of God, did not consider it robbery to be equal with God.' (Philippians 2.5-6).

Is the church ready for the second coming of the Lord? No! Is the church prepared for the final and the next/last move of God? The answer is definitely no. The last move of God will be the final fulfilment of every prophecy, final demonstration of the fullness of God's power. It is something we have not seen before. So the last move of God might not have a reference point. Are we ready for it? No, we are not.

There is no doubt that the last days began with the first outpouring of the Holy Spirit. "And it shall come to pass in the last days,' says God, 'that I will pour out of My Spirit on all flesh." After 2,000 years into this dispensation, we have come to the last of the last days. Six days are almost complete. We are very close to the seventh day of rest. The rebirth of the nation of Israel, the return of the Jews to Israel, and the prosperity of Israel point to the fact that the end is very close. The prophecy of the end time by Daniel says that it shall be a time of trouble such as never was before. 'And shall be a time of trouble, such as never was since there was a nation … but you, Daniel, shut up the words, and seal the book until the time of the end; many shall run to and fro, and knowledge shall increase … Many shall be purified, and made white and refined but the wicked shall do wickedly.' (Daniel 12.1-10). This is the time we are in. The present information technology is unparalleled in human history.

Now the tracts of the 'time of trouble' are being laid unnoticeably. Christians have begun to face persecutions in places where Christianity had been the bedrock of their culture and civilisation. Jesus Himself said, 'And then many will be offended, will betray one another, and will hate one another … and because lawlessness will abound the love of many will grow cold.' Paul says,

'But know this, that in the last days perilous times will come; for men will be lovers of themselves, lovers of money, boasters, proud, blasphemers, disobedient to parents, unthankful, unholy, unloving, unforgiving, slanderers, without self-control, brutal, despisers of good, traitors, headstrong, haughty, lovers of pleasure rather than lovers of God, having a form of godliness but denying its power. And from such people turn away.'

2Tim 3.1-5

Yes, wickedness and evil have increased very much in our world and in our churches. Many churches and people who call themselves Christians speak a form of the gospel but deny its power. It will be as if the spirits of Cain, Nimrod, Ammon, Esau, and Absalom are revisiting our world and our churches. As people get further and further away from the presence of God, so do occult practices increase. Occultism now fills our schools, entertainment, and our music. Our television is already full of the occult if you care to look. The devil is systematically indoctrinating us and desensitising us through the major media outlets.

Truth is cast aside as untruth while deceit flourish and is applauded. Apostle Paul says, 'They are always learning and never able to come to the knowledge of the truth.' He also says, 'Now the

Spirit expressly says that in latter times some will depart from the faith, giving heed to deceiving spirits and doctrines of demons.' (Timothy 4.1). It is not so difficult to get corrupted in Christian meetings and churches today. Satanic meetings/churches are allowed by governments.

The world and the flesh fight against the church and the Spirit, just as Ishmael fought against Isaac. The spirit and the system of antichrist are becoming stronger and stronger. Opposition to the Biblical truth is coming from all sorts of corners even among Christians themselves. Many Christians have fallen away, back-slidden; while others are in religious and entertainment mode and while others are in despair. The church has become fleshy and lost much of its kingdom power and the gospel is being commercialised. The devil is using the church against the church. Yes, things will be and are going to be very bad, very impossible in the last of the last days.

CHAPTER 12

The Sound Of Abundance Of Rain

The greatest question people are beginning to ask is 'What is going to be the next move of God after the Charismatic Revival?' I have tried to portray the state of the present church as I see it in the last chapter, in order to expose the fact that the church is not ready for the next revival or the next move of God. We even pray for revival, but we are the obstacles to revival. In the state we are in, we shall be the first to fight the next revival and the last move of God when it comes.

This last revival and move of God will have no precedence and no reference point. 'Eye has not seen, nor ear heard, nor have entered into the heart of man the things which God has prepared for those who love him.' The last move or the outpouring will be such that unless believers are walking with the Spirit, they are the very people who will reject it and attribute it to witchcraft and devils.

God will shake the church until there is a remnant or His bride has made herself ready. "Yet once more I shake not only the earth, but also the heaven.' Now this, 'Yet once more', indicates the removal of those things that are being shaken, as of things that are made, that the things which cannot be shaken may remain. Therefore, since we are receiving a kingdom which cannot be shaken, let us have grace, by which we may serve God acceptably with reverence and godly fear. For God is a consuming fire.' (Hebrews 12.26–29).

This warning is coming right after the discourse of Mount Zion. 'See that you do not refuse Him who speaks. For if they did not escape who refused Him who spoke on earth, much more shall we not escape if we turn away from Him who speak from heaven.' (Hebrews 12.25). How many voices are speaking on Mount Zion? Eight! Heaven is speaking, let us tune in to listen.

The church will be the first to be shaken because judgement will begin with her (1 Peter 4.17). The shaking might take many forms, like persecution of churches and oppression from earthly governments and other faiths. Church may be left empty, folded up, or just dwindle away because it is no longer useful. The Holy Spirit may choose to retire some ministers or call them home. Call it 'wilderness' or 'tribulation,' but something will happen that will weed out the half-baked Christians, the unfaithful and the fleshy Christians and leave the remnant or the bride. 'Those who love their souls will lose them.' Looking at the carnal church of today, the demonic cultic system and the antichrist systems in the world, the apostasy and the rebellion to the gospel of the kingdom, the Last Move of God will touch every sphere of human life.

Prophet Isaiah says, 'For behold, the darkness shall cover the earth, and deep darkness the people; but the Lord will arise over you, and the glory will be seen upon you. The Gentiles shall come to your light, and the kings to the brightness of your rising.' (Isaiah 60.2-3). Right in the time of trouble, gloom, evil, wickedness and darkness, the Lord will arise over his people and the glory of God will be seen over them. The gentiles will be attracted to the remnant because of the glory of God upon her. This is how the last harvest will be reaped. First the glory of the Lord will come upon the remnant, the bride of Christ in the age of darkness, gloom, need, lack, wickedness, evil etc. Then the gentiles will see the light on God's people and come over to the kingdom. The remnant shall be the repository of the greatest glory of God. The last revival and the move of God is going to flow from us believers. What Jesus said will be fulfilled in its fullest. 'Out of your heart will flow rivers of living waters.'

Apostle Paul says, talking about Jesus, 'And He gave some to be apostles, some prophets, some evangelists and some pastors and teachers, for the equipping of the saints for the work of the ministry, for the edifying of the body of Christ, till we all come to the unity of the faith and the knowledge of the Son of God, to a perfect man, to the measure of the stature of the fullness of Christ.' (Ephesians 4.11-13). Jesus gave His resurrected abilities to individuals to prepare and equip ordinary believers to minister to the world. These offices cannot build the church without the ordinary believers. This plan of God seems thwarted by the five-fold ministers themselves and by the religious atmosphere in many churches.

Apostle Paul also says the church is built on the foundation of the apostles and the prophets with Jesus Christ as the chief corner stone (Ephesians 2.20). Some churches do not have apostles and prophets anyway. Those which have these offices have not largely operated in such a way to equip the saints. I have seen only few places where believers are trained and empowered. Many times, the gifted ministers use their gifts in such a way that the people put their trust in them instead of God. Without the ministers the people look powerless. Many believers feel unequipped and helpless to minister to the world. In the next move of God, ordinary believers will be so gifted by the Holy Spirit that it will put the office holders to shame.

Apostle Paul further gave an indication that the five-fold ministry will give way to a new generation; 'till we all come …' The new generation will be the age of the matured sons of God. They may not be Pastors, Apostles or prophets. They may not have any titles, but do not mess about with them, because even creation will recognise and obey them. 'For the earnest expectation of the creation eagerly waits for the revealing of the sons of God. For the creation was subjected to futility, not willingly, but because of Him who subjected it in hope.' (Romans 8.19-20).

When this new generation comes into being there will be no need for the five-fold ministry. If the office holders are not transformed into sons, their ministries will be irrelevant. You know what, the professional five-fold office holders will be the first to fight against this new generation. God is preparing His army for the end time; people who would carry His glory and anointing for awesome and unbelievable miracles.

God has not told me the name of this new movement after the five-fold ministry. But the fact is that Christ preached and taught only one message: the gospel of the kingdom. In the 40 days that He was on the earth after His resurrection, He taught His apostles things pertaining to the kingdom of God. Furthermore, He prophesied that, 'This gospel of the kingdom will be preached in all the world as a witness to all the nations, and then the end will come.' (Matthew 24.14). The remnant and the sons must correctly pick up the baton of the gospel of the kingdom of God again and carry it to the finish line. It might therefore be a kingdom movement or a kingdom oriented. It does not matter which name is given, but it will have a sonship foundation.

There are two Greek words used for sons in the New Testament. The first is the Greek word, *'teknon.' 'But as many as receive Him, to them he gave the right to become the children [sons] of God, to those who believe in His name.' (John 1.12). 'The Spirit Himself bears witness with our spirit that we are the children [sons] of God.' (Romans 8.16). Teknon means the mere fact of birth, like a biological son. This is the spiritual rebirth or regeneration and makes one a natural heir. But the child may not inherit, take dominion or rule because of immaturity. 'Now I say that the heir, as long as he is a child, does not differ at all from a slave, though he is master of all but is under guardians and stewards until the time appointed by the father.' (Galatians 4.1-2). A child of God must be spiritually trained and processed through time.*

The second Greek word translated as sons is 'huios.' 'You are My beloved Son; in You I am well pleased'. Huios is a son identifiable by the character or the characteristics of the father. He is like the father and behaves like Him. This is the son of adoption. 'Having predestined us to adoption as sons by Jesus Christ to Himself, according to the good pleasure of His will.' (Ephesians 1.5). The Greek word adoption is 'huiothesia,' a derivative of huios. We are spiritual sons who possess the spirit of adoption in our hearts that we may cry, 'Abba, Father.'

'For as many as are led by the Spirit of God, these are the sons of God.' (Romans 8.14). The Greek word is huios. To be led by the Spirit of God one needs the light of God. The light of God, from the menorah, is found in the Holy Place of the tabernacle of Moses and not in the outer court. The pattern was that only the priest went to the Holy Place. So, one cannot be a true son, practically, without being a priest. Every believer is a priest according to the order of Melchizedek, but we need to enter the Holy Place and function as a priest. That is the only way to be led by the Spirit of God.

'Now after six days Jesus took Peter, James and John his brother, led them up on a high mountain by themselves; and he was transfigured before them. His face shone like the sun, and His clothes became as white as the light.' (Matthew 17.1-2). Now six days of creation are over and we are expecting to be ushered into the seventh day of rest. Jesus Christ on the mountain was transfigured and became light. And a voice suddenly came out of the cloud saying, 'This is my Beloved Son, in whom I am well pleased. Hear Him!' (Matthew 17.5). At the baptism of Jesus at Jordan the Father identified a priestly Son. 'This is my Beloved Son, in whom I am well pleased.' But on the mountain, the Father identified a matured and exalted Son. One who has inherited all the Father has. Hear Him! Now the sea will hear, the rivers will hear, the wind will hear, famine will hear, disease will hear, the devil will hear etc. Creation will now hear Him (Romans 8.19). Jesus led Peter, James and John to a high mountain. The highest spiritual mountain for believers is Mount Zion (Hebrews 12.22).

Prophet Elijah challenged the prophets of Baal and Asherah on Mount Carmel. Let's see what happened at the time of the evening sacrifice. The prophets of Baal and Asherah did all they could from morning to evening without any result. 'And when midday was past, they prophesied until the time of the offering of the evening sacrifice. But there was no voice, no one answered, no one paid attention.'

The evening sacrifice was the last sacrifice and corresponds to the last prayer/worship of the day. I believe the evening sacrifice points to the end time. It shows that at the last revival the fire of God will fall again, and it gives credence to the fact that the fire angels, seraphim, and the cherubim will pay us visits during the end time.

When the fire fell and the people turned to God, Elijah said, 'Go up, eat and drink; for there is the sound of the abundance of rain.' (1 Kings 18.41). It had not rained for three and half years and the nation was in serious need and famine; so it shall be in the time of Tribulation. Elijah went to the top of Mount Carmel to pray. Still no rain. He sent his servant seven times to check the cloud for signs of rain. Still no rain! 'Then it came to pass the seventh time, that he said, 'There is a cloud, as small as a man's hand, rising out of the sea.' So he said, 'Go up, say to Ahab, Prepare your chariot, and go down before the rain stops you." (1 Kings 18.41).

1 Kings 18.45-46

We have already mentioned that rainfall is a picture of the out-pouring of the Spirit of God. This rainfall was another shadow of the prophecy of Joel for the restoration of the Jews from the curse of the locust, that there will be an unusual heavy rainfall in the end time. When the rain started, the Spirit of God fell upon Elijah. He girded his loins and outran Ahab, who was being driven by chariots. Humanly speaking it was impossible, but spiritually it was a type of translocation. This I believe will also be common in the end time.

Before Elijah was taken up into heaven, he asked his servant Elisha, 'Ask! What may I do for you, before I am taken away from you?' Elisha said, 'Please let a double portion of your spirit be upon me.' (2 Kings 2.9). Elijah did not have what Elisha was asking for. But as a son Elisha had the right to receive the double portion of his father's possession. Elijah replied, 'You have asked a hard thing. Nevertheless, if you see me when I am taken from you, it shall be so for you; but if not, it shall not be so.' As I pondered on the reply of Elijah, the Lord directed me to Acts 1.9-11.

Acts 1.9-11

Then I remembered, the 'powers of the age to come.' It dawned on me that the remnant in the last days would operate in a far greater power and anointing than Elijah. Elijah knew that such double anointing was slated for the end time. If Elisha could tap into the age of the end time, he could receive what he was asking for; otherwise, it was not possible. So the double portion of the spirit and power of Elijah is going to be upon some people, the Elishas, in the end time. When Elisha saw Elijah been taken up into heaven, he cried, 'My father, my father, the chariot of Israel and its horsemen!' Elijah left his mantle for Elisha, but Elisha did not leave his mantle to anyone, because it was for the end time generation.

'Behold, I will send you Elijah the prophet before the coming of the great and dreadful day of the Lord. And he will turn the hearts of the fathers to the children and the hearts of the children to their fathers lest I come and strike the earth with a curse.' (Malachi 4.5-6). In the last of the last days God will raise the Elijahs, who will operate in the spirit and powers of Elijah. He will also raise the Elishas, who will operate in the double portion or far greater anointing than the Elijahs and make the path of the Lord straight again. Jesus confirmed that John the Baptist came in the spirit and power of Elijah to prepare for His earthly ministry (Matthew 11.7-19). John the Baptist said,

> *'A man can receive nothing unless it has been given to him from heaven. You yourselves bear me witness that I said, 'I am not the Christ, but I have been sent before him.' He who has the bride is the bridegroom; but the friend of the bridegroom, who stands and hears him, rejoices greatly because of the bridegroom's voice. Therefore this joy of mine is fulfilled.'*
>
> John 3.27-29

One of the definitions given by the Thayer Dictionary is that the friend of the bridegroom, on his behalf, asks the hand of the bride and renders him various services to close the marriage and the celebration of the nuptials. The bride we know is the body of the *ekklesia* who has made herself ready, and the bridegroom we know is Jesus Christ. Who is the friend of the bridegroom?

The friend rejoices when the bridegroom appears, and John the Baptist says his joy was fulfilled at the appearance of Jesus

Christ. So John the Baptist was implying that he was a friend of Jesus Christ. We have to know the ministry of John the Baptist to understand the role of a friend of Jesus in the last days. Angel Gabriel prophesied of John the Baptist to his father Zechariah.

> 'He will also be filled with the Holy Spirit, even from his mother's womb. And he will turn many of the children of Israel to the Lord their God. He will also go before Him in the spirit and power of Elijah, to turn the hearts of the fathers to the children and the disobedient to the wisdom of the just, to make ready a people prepared for the Lord.'
>
> Luke 1.15-7

First, the anointing upon John the Baptist would remove the separation between mankind and Jesus Christ. Second, John the Baptist would work in the spirit and power of Elijah to also remove the separation between the fathers and their sons. Elijah would turn the hearts of the fathers to their children, and the hearts of the children to their fathers (Malachi 4.6).

The 'fathers' refer to those who had or have had the promises and the covenants of God and kept them. So far as the fathers were spiritually separated from their children, the children would be excluded from the promises and the covenants. In such a case the plan of God would be defeated and there would not have been any need for Jesus Christ to come, because the generation of the people in His day would not be qualified to connect to the promises and the covenants of God. I refer especially to God's promises and covenants with Abraham, through whose seed the whole of mankind was to be blessed.

In the same way, the fathers of the gospel, like Apostle Peter, Apostle John, and Apostle Paul, have to connect to the children of this generation despite the great differences in culture in order to be aligned with what they walked in. Elijah would come again, to restore and heal the separation and the brokenness of people in our day and give them a chance to receive the grace of God through Jesus Christ and fulfil all the promises of God.

Zechariah, the father of John the Baptist, also prophesised at the birth of John the Baptist.

Luke 1.76-79

John the Baptist, the friend of Jesus Christ, had to come in advance, in the spirit and power of Elijah, to prepare people for salvation through Jesus Christ, to point to Christ as the Anointed One and to lead people in darkness and under the shadow of death to Jesus Christ, the Light of the world, the Life and the Prince of Peace. He pointed to Jesus Christ and said, 'Behold! The lamb of God who takes away the sin of the world.'

John the Baptist began to preach in the wilderness of Judea, saying, 'Repent, for the kingdom of heaven is at hand.' He went into all the region around Jordan, preaching the baptism of repentance for the remission of sins, 'as it is written in the book of the words of Isaiah the prophet,' saying:

Luke 3.3-5

John the Baptist was trained by God in the wilderness. The gospel of Mark says that he was clothed with camel's hair and with a leather belt around his waist, and he ate locusts and wild honey. He came from a priestly family but did not dress like one of them; neither did he choose to remain in the temple and enjoy the privileges of the priests of his day. He disciplined himself through the harsh conditions of the wilderness in simple life. John the Baptist stayed in the wilderness until his anointing was mature and when he started his ministry, he caused a revival in his region.

For 400 years God was silent, there was no Voice and no prophet. Suddenly, the voice of God rang out loud in the wilderness through John the Baptist, 'Repent, the kingdom of heaven is at hand,' then Jerusalem, all Judea and all the region around Jordan went to him and followed the Voice of God from a simple holy man. They confessed their sins and were baptised. The people he preached to were Jews, the people of God who had the word, the oracle, and the covenants. To them all other people, the non-Jews, were sinners. But John the Baptist did not preach to the non-Jews; instead, he preached to the Jews as sinners, even though they were obeying the Law of Moses.

When the Pharisees and the Sadducees, the religious leaders, came to his baptism, he said to them, 'Brood of vipers! Who warned you to flee from the wrath to come? Therefore bear fruits worthy of repentance, and do not think to say to yourselves, 'We have Abraham as our father.' For I say to you that God is able to raise up children to Abraham from these stones. And even now the axe is laid to the root of the tree. Therefore every tree which does not bear good fruit is cut down and thrown into the fire.' (Matthew 3.7-10).

Among friends the rigid barriers of protocol are broken down. A friend is someone one can easily talk to and share intimate secrets. A friend may not be your father, your child, or your spouse. You can be born again, spirit-filled, anointed, a very successful minister and still not be a friend of Christ. Friends constantly commune in fellowship and share secrets. God is concerned about what is happening in our churches today and I believe He wants friends He can speak to, like he spoke to Enoch, the seventh patriarch, about the second coming of Jesus, 6,000 years before it actually happened, like Noah, like Abraham and like Moses.

Jesus Christ said to His disciples, 'You are My friends if you do whatever I command you. No longer do I call you servants, for a servant does not know what his master is doing; but I have called you friends, for all things that I heard from My Father I have made known to you.' (John 15.14-15). The disciples were moved to the next level of relationship with Jesus Christ. 'You are My friends.' Our personal relationship with Jesus is very important. Whom you relate to and are intimate with will determine your victory or your defeat.

The end time anointing and/or the 'powers of the age to come' will be on the friends of Jesus Christ for the end time harvest, preparing the bride of Jesus, training and protecting her before Jesus returns. The friends of Jesus Christ will be able to live in both realms of the spirit and of the earth and shall have such tremendous supernatural powers to withstand and to help others to withstand the great darkness, depression, and desolation of the end time. They shall also help to fulfil every promise, every covenant, and every purpose of God.

It will not only be people with the spirit of Elijah and Elisha, but also people with the anointing or the spirit of Moses, Joseph, Enoch, Joshua, Jeremiah, Ezekiel, Apostle Paul, Apostle John, and many of the saints of faith in heaven. They will all be instrumental in the end time. 'God having provided something better for us, that they should not be made perfect apart from us.' (Hebrews 11.40). 'They' refers to the people of faith, some of whom are mentioned in Hebrews chapter 11. These glorious saints in heaven will come and join themselves with us to complete their destiny and their assignments. It will be a time of unprecedented manifestation of the glory of God, in such a way that, unless people are in the Spirit, they will not embrace it. What people do not believe they will not understand. What they do not understand they cannot receive. What they cannot receive, they will fight it.

We have to be careful we do not reject the very revival we have been praying and fasting for over the years.

Prophet Isaiah prophesied seven spirits which rested upon Jesus Christ; the Spirit of the Lord, the spirit of wisdom, spirit of understanding, the spirit of counsel, spirit of might, the spirit of knowledge and the spirit of the fear of the Lord. These are not seven gifts of the Holy Spirit, but they are seven spirits. Each one is symbolised by the colours of the rainbow. When the colours of a rainbow are blended together, they become white light. So, the seven spirits lend their characters or powers and blend together to achieve a glorious purpose of God. I believe the same spirits worked with the early church fathers to do mighty signs and wonders in their ministries. Though the powers come from God, they are executed through spirits or angels. I also believe that in the end time the same seven spirits will be fully active in the lives of many believers to train and equip them to fully attain to the stature of matured sons of light, in order to appropriate fully the powers of the kingdom of God.

In the past 50 years the church has seen restoration of different gifts of the Holy Spirit, healing, teaching, evangelism, intercessory gifts, prophetic gifts, and apostolic gifts. These might have been the joint effort of the seven spirits of God and angels working directly with us. These seven spirits are also portrayed in the book of Revelation. In Revelations 4.5 are 'the seven lamps of fire burning before the throne.' In Revelations 5.6 are 'the seven horns and the seven ayes, which are the seven spirits of God sent out into all the earth.' These really are part of the glory of God. So, in the last move of God, the activities of these spirits will be very important to the saints on earth.

Seven is the number of fullness and completion, so in the last move of God, before Jesus returns, these seven spirits will be released in their fullness. First will be the seven lamps of fire before the throne of God, which will expose the full radiance and brightness of God in a way we have not seen before. The slightest sin or darkness will therefore be exposed. These lamps are also the spirits of fire. Fire cleanses, separates, enlightens, tests, refines, purifies, consumes, destroys, sanctifies, consecrates, and empowers. These spirits of lamps and fire will release their attributes in their fullness to anoint, purify, consecrate, destroy and consume in a level we have not seen before. They shall cover and judge the holiness of God. So, in the last move of God the holiness of God will be a major issue, as it was at the beginning of His relationship with the children of Israel. The occurrence of Ananias and Sapphira, who died before the glory of God, will be a common phenomenon.

In Revelations 5.6, the Lamb, which was the symbol of Christ, had seven horns and seven eyes, which are the seven spirits of God. The horn is always the symbol of strength, power, and dominion. These seven horn spirits will work with the matured sons of God to have full strength, full power, and full dominion in every situation. It will be crucial for the survival of the saints in the end time during the time of the antichrist system and the time of Tribulation.

There will also be the seven eye spirits, which will be released upon the matured sons and work with them to have full prophetic powers. Nothing will be hidden from them, so the last move of God will see people with far greater prophetic anointing and ministries. Perhaps we are beginning to see these in some ministers. But in the end time many shall operate in such capacities.

You can see, from the cursory picture of the church I have painted above, that the church needs a thorough cleansing and purification before the Second Coming of Jesus Christ. 'But who can endure the day of His coming? And who can stand when He appears? For He is like a refiner's fire and like launderers' soap. He will sit as a refiner and a purifier of silver; He will purify the sons of Levi, and purge them as gold and silver, that they may offer to the Lord an offering in righteousness ... And I will come near you for judgement; I will be a swift witness against sorcerers, against adulterers, against perjurers, against those who exploits wage earners and widows and orphans, and against those who turn away an alien – because they do not fear Me.' (Malachi 3.2-5). Many Churches and Christians who are not prepared shall not survive the purifier and the refiner's fire in the last days.

The Bible says that the time has come for judgement to begin in the house of God (1 Peter 4.17). When it begins the Pastors, Prophets, Apostles, Bishops, and other ministers will be the first on the list. The coming judgement will take many forms, fire, persecution, trials, attacks, battles, earthquakes, famine, etc. and will take away every pollution and every uncleanliness from the church until the bride (church) is ready and well adorned. 'Husbands love your wives just as Christ also loved the church and gave Himself for her that He might sanctify and cleanse her with the washing of water by the word, that he might present her to himself a glorious church, not having spot or wrinkle or any such thing, but that she should be holy and without blemish.' (Ephesians 5.23-25).

Jesus warns us Himself, 'As it was in the days of Noah, so it will be also in the days of the Son of Man ... until the day that Noah entered the ark then the flood came and destroyed them all.' (Luke 17.26-27). Noah was a just man, perfect in his generation, and walked with God (Genesis 6.9). 'Likewise as it was also in the days of Lot ... on the day that Lot went out of Sodom it rained fire and brimstone from heaven and destroyed them all.' (Luke 17.28-29). Both Noah and Lot were referred to as righteous men. And both were saved from God's judgement. They were not raptured but saved from the judgements.

Over the years we have taken for granted the holiness of the Lord, especially the Charismatic Movement. The time is coming soon when the holiness of God will once again burn like a consuming fire. As it was in the beginning so it shall be in the end. Remember Uzzah touched the ark of God, and God struck him dead for his error. Remember Nadab and Abihu, who took profane fire before the Lord, and the fire of the Lord consumed them. The people of Beth Shemesh looked into the Ark of the Covenant, and in one flash 50,070 men died. God warned Aaron, 'By those who come near Me I must be regarded as holy; and before all the people I must be glorified.' (Leviticus 10.1-3). Remember Ananias and Sapphira, who died instantly before the apostles in the church for their lies and hypocrisy. These were all warnings for us to whom the end has come. It is definite that the fire of God's holiness will come again and when it comes it will be seven times more powerful and deadly. The last move of God will purify some churches and some Christians, but it will also consume and destroy some churches and some Christians.

In the last move of God, I believe the seraphim Isaiah saw in Isaiah chapter six will come back. Isaiah saw seraphim above the throne of God; he did not tell us their number, but the vision of prophet Daniel states, 'A thousand thousands ministered to Him; ten thousand times ten thousand stood before Him.' (Daniel 7.10). So there might have been plenty of seraphim above the throne of God. Seraphim means 'burning ones' or 'fiery ones.' One of the seraphim took a live coal from the altar and touched Isaiah's lips with it and said, 'Behold, this has touched your lips; your iniquity is taken away, and you sin purged.' (Isaiah 6.6-7). These special angelic beings keep and protect the holiness of God.

The fire of the seraphim will come back to expose every uncleanness, the hidden sins and the counterfeits in the church and also purify the penitent hearts to bring transformation. Some churches and some people will be hit by the fire of transformation to prepare them for the coming glory of God, while others will perish. The seraphim transformed Isaiah's motives, priorities, intentions, and desires. In the last move of God these fiery angelic beings will be very active to change our fleshy motives, priorities, intentions, and desires and prepare people to receive the glory of God.

In the throne room experience of Ezekiel, there were four cherubim connected with the glory of God. Cherubim are special angelic beings which carry and protect/cover the glory of God. I do not believe God created only four of them. I believe they represent a company of them, four of which Ezekiel saw. These special angelic beings will also be prominent in the last move of God. 'Where the Spirit went, they also went.' God will release the cherubim in the last days to bring the glory of God to those who are prepared and ready for it.

In the midst of persecution, desolation, darkness, violence, evil, wickedness and seemingly impossible situations, the church will birth the end time remnant who will live under open heaven and carry extraordinary and incredible kingdom powers of our time.

It is clear from what I have said so far that in the last move of God, the glory of God will not be for special people or necessarily people in one location. God will use people all over the world who have made themselves ready. It will not be necessary to go to the USA, England, or Wales or Azusa Street to experience the move of God; it will be all over the world. God is going to use a lot of people we do not know about. The glory of God will flow from countless number of people. We shall be carriers of the manifest glory of God. This is where we are heading to. 'The earth shall be filled with the knowledge of the glory of the Lord as the waters cover the sea.' I feel belittled by God's goodness and His plan for the end time.

Paul confirms this, 'In the dispensation of the fullness of times He might gather together in one all things in Christ, both which are in heaven and those which are on earth – in Him.' (Ephesians 1.10). And angel Gabriel updated Prophet Daniel about the end time.

*'Seventy weeks are determined for your people and for the holy city, to finish
the transgression, to make an end of sins, to make reconciliation for iniquity, to
bring in everlasting righteousness, to seal up visions and prophecy and to anoint
the Most Holy.'*

Daniel 9.24

In the last move of God every sin, transgression and iniquity will
be judged or purged. Every word God has spoken will be fulfilled and there will be everlasting righteousness. The last outpouring or the last move of the Holy Spirit will complete the plan
of God and complete the restoration of what man lost through
the first Adam. It will be the time when the former rain and the
later rain will be in one month.

Jerusalem Pentecost did not end the prophecy of Joel but set up
the stage for the next two major outpourings of the Holy Spirit.
'I will show wonders in the heavens and in the earth; blood and
fire and pillar of smoke. The sun shall be turned into darkness
and the moon into blood, before the coming of the great and
awesome day of the Lord. And it shall come to pass that whoever calls on the name of the Lord shall be saved. For in Mount
Zion and in Jerusalem there shall be deliverance, as the Lord has
said, among the remnant whom the Lord calls.' (Joel 2.30-32,
Acts 2.19-21). In the last move of God there will be wonders in
heaven and earth.

Activities of Angels and other members of the family of God will
be common-place. Translocation will be widespread and common knowledge, as in the life of Elijah. We are in this special age
when many of these phenomena have started happening already.
I believe we are the last generation before the Lord comes back.

The latter rain (the Azusa Street Revival) was heavier than the
former rain (Jerusalem Pentecost). Prophet Haggai's well-known
prophesy says, 'the glory of this latter temple shall be greater than
the former.' The third and the last Pentecost is on the way. This

last move of God or the Last Outpouring of the Holy Spirit will be far greater than that of the early church. Because of what the early church did and what they achieved with the initial gifts, I am speechless and find it difficult, almost impossible, to imagine and put into words with certainty what the fullness of the 'powers of the age to come' will be, or the extent of the last move of God.

While praying and fasting, God opened my eyes and I saw an outpouring of rain upon what looked like a metal container. The rainfall stopped; after a few seconds it started again, but this time it was like water pebbles/small snowballs. The Outpouring had deepened, intensified, and concentrated. That also stopped. After about 30 minutes, the vision came back. This time the rainfall was very heavy and profuse. Instead of water or snowballs I saw what looked like small fish raining on the earth with great ferocity. Then I realised it was a vision of the end time harvest of souls. I saw a black and white map of so many countries, each with its name, but I could not read the names properly. One of the maps I saw resembled that of USA. So, I put it in my journal: 'The end time harvest of souls will not be at a corner but affect nations.'

Be ready.

God bless you.

The author

Solomon S. Aggrey is a Bible Teacher and Preacher originally from Cape Coast, Ghana. He was ordained into the Anglican Communion in Nigeria and is now Head Pastor at the Temple of Shalom Christian Church in Manchester, United Kingdom. He has two adult children and enjoys reading and writing. This is his authorial debut.